Self Psychology in the Select Novels of Arun Joshi and Kiran Desai

Self Psychology in the Select Novels of Arun Joshi and Kiran Desai

Kavitha Raj

Book Title: Self Psychology in the Select Novels of Arun Joshi And Kiran Desai
Book Author: Dr. K. Kavitharaj
Published by SMART MOVES
E 5/11, 2nd Floor, Bitten Market
Bhopal-462038, M.P, India

Printed and bound by SMART MOVES
E 5/11, 2nd Floor, Bitten Market
Bhopal-462038, M.P, India
 e-ISBN- 978-81-935930-7-3
p-ISBN-978-81-935930-8-0
This edition published in: 2018 ISBN (ISBN Pending)

Contents

Foreword

The book titled "Self Psychology in the Select Novels of Arun Joshi and Kiran Desai" is a comprehensive effort made with interest and dedication by Dr K Kavitharaj. I would like to convey my special appreciation to the author's sincere and innovative research, especially in the topic of Self Psychology proposed by Heinz Kohut. The theme of the book is entirely new to the readers as it deals with theories of modern Psychoanalysis rooted from Freud's Psychoanalysis. It also philosophically gives an understanding of what life is in this materialistic world of money and power through the characters of the select novels of Arun Joshi and Kiran Desai. The work is original and has a compete line of thought. It explores various other concepts and theories of further studies for researchers.

I wish the author all the best for her work and expect further such quality publication from her in future.

Dr. V Umadevi

Assistant Professor
Post Graduate and Research
Department of English
Government Arts College, Coimbatore

Preface

The book is a fine version of my Ph. D thesis which is the outcome of my research in English where I analysed the theory of Self Psychology in two sets of comparative analysis in the select novels of Arun Joshi and Kiran Desai. I always have a bent towards theories and that inspired me to do my research on the theory of Self Psychology. I opted this theory as it is not only descriptive or simply theoretical, it is applicable in our day to day life and can be analysed on any human beings of any traits.

The studies are usually done on the theme of self like how the characters lose their identity due to social barriers and how they regain and retain their self. In the book, study is related to the theme of self which is illustrated based on one of the psychoanalytic theories namely Self Psychology which is a prominent theory for psychoanalytic therapy and treatment that is widely accepted and practiced all over the world. The theory rooted from Psychoanalysis patterns the reasons for the disorder in self and the ways to develop or form a cohesive self.

The book would change the mindset of researchers on Theories and would give them ample ideas on psychoanalytic theories which could be applied on any characters. The third and fourth chapter of this book would run like a story where the readers can relate themselves and persons around them with the characters in the novels. The book as a whole would impress upon what cohesive self is or in other words how to live a life of being accepted by others in a social set up and what makes them unable to attain it.

Introduction

Self is the conception that should be unique in any individual to live a meaningful and complete life which makes him to prove his real attitude and his mutual relationship with the world. Living a life of being a socially acceptable and recognized personality of some use to others serves the purpose even in this materialistic life. It is obvious that there are human values and morals which form the basis for mankind as a whole in the past, present and even in the future. Hence the importance ofSelf is explained in this book based on the theory of Self Psychology proposed by Heinz Kohut in 1960s. The theory is applied on the two sets of comparative analysis of the select novels of Arun Joshi and Kiran Desai.

Literature is the reflection of life and so the characters in the novels may resemble or reflect men in general where he runs for money, power and material. But at the end of his life, it is hard to find happiness and peace. So this book would give an idea of what self is, what makes men to live a pathetic meaningless life and what are the ways to live a life of cohesive self of use to others. Living together and being an acceptable person in the society in which we live would really make us feel the worth of being born in this beautiful world. So this book would give the reasons for disorder self and cohesive self amidst individuals to live a better optimistic life.

1

Introduction

Introduction

What a disturbing contrast there is between the radiant intelligence of the child and the feeble mentality of the average adult.

Sigmund Freud

Self is the conception that marks the uniqueness of an individual from others. It makes him to prove his real attitude and his mutual relationship with the world. It actually provides energy to an individual to face his life, both success and failure in an optimistic way. Ultimately the life should make men feel the completeness of living treasuring the sweet memories of his life of being a socially acceptable and recognized personality of use to others. Obviously this completeness, happiness and acceptability is all life about which makes the real difference among individuals in spite of other diversities like nation, religion, race, culture, regulations etc. There are number of studies on the theme of self like how the characters lose their identity due to social barriers and how they regain and retain their self. But the present study is related to the theme of self which is illustrated or substantiated based on one of the psychoanalytic theories namely Self Psychology proposed by Heinz Kohut, which is a prominent theory for psychoanalytic therapy and treatment that is widely accepted and practiced all over the world.

The theory of Self Psychology is applied on two sets of comparative studies to demonstrate the major concept of Self Psychology: the first is that of Arun Joshi's *The StrangeCase of Billy Biswas* and Kiran Desai's *Hullabaloo in the Guava Orchard* where the protagonists depict the manifestation of the disorder in self and the second is that of Arun Joshi's *The Apprentice* and Kiran Desai's *The Inheritance of Loss* where the characters though in the beginning were unable to retain their self, due to their social background and barriers, towards the end of the novel, they realize the significance of living a meaningful life of use to others and to be a socially acceptable person. This realization is the result of their development of cohesive self as formulated by Heinz Kohut in his theory of Self Psychology. Heinz Kohut remarks the potentials of a person with cohesive self as; A person experiences himself as a cohesive, harmonious unit in space and time which is connected with its past and directed toward a creative and productive future, [but] only if he has the experience at every stage of his life that certain representatives of his human environment react enthusiastically to him, are available as sources of idealized strength and calm, present in nursing, but essentially always able to understand his inner life more or less correctly so that their reactions and his needs are in tune and he is permitted to comprehend their inner life if he requires such support. (84)

Introduction to Psychoanalysis

The root of Self Psychology is psychoanalysis which is a specific mind investigation technique and therapy which is closer to psychotherapy and farther from philosophical speculation inspired from investigations. It is a set of psychological and psychotherapeutic theories and associated techniques, created by Austrian physician Sigmund Freud and stemming partly from the clinical work of Josef Breuer and others. It is a discipline which is based on the knowledge acquired from applying the investigation method and clinical experiences. Freud himself was very clear on this point that he changed the very conception of human nature. Freud's mastery was remarked by Hilgard in his *Introduction to Psychology* as:

Of course, the progress of science will by its very nature correct popular misunderstandings of how the world works, and occasionally reveal surprising, even unpleasant, truths about ourselves. Sigmund Freud famously situated himself in line with Copernicus, who taught us that Earth is not at the center of the universe, and Darwin, who taught us that humans are creatures of nature just like any other. For Freud, the third blow against 'human megalomania' was his discovery (as he claimed it was) that conscious experience, thought, and action was determined by unconscious, primitive drives. (285)

Sigmund Freud was a Jewish neuro pathologist who tried to set up a psychoanalytical movement in order to make his orientation more reliable. He lived most of his life in Vienna and died in London in 1939. He discovered psychoanalysis by systematizing ideas and information derived from different theoretical and clinical directions. The self-analysis, to which Freud was submitted himself, represented the biggest contribution to the birth of psychoanalysis. Two Encyclopedia Article in 1923 has marked Psychoanalysis as the name of a procedure for the investigation of mental processes which are almost inaccessible in any other way. It is a methodfor the treatment of neurotic disorders and a collection of psychological information obtained along those lines, which is gradually being accumulated into a new scientific discipline.

The basic tenets of psychoanalysis include that a person's development is determined by forgotten events in his early childhood rather than by his inherited traits alone. It is demonstrated that human attitude, mannerism, experience and thought are largely influenced by irrational drives that are basically rooted in the unconscious. It is essential to by-pass psychological resistance in the form of defense mechanisms in order to bring drives into awareness. Also the conflicts between the conscious and the unconscious or with repressed material can materialize in the form of mental or emotional disturbances, for example: neurosis, neurotic traits, anxiety, depression etc. It is also illustrated that to liberate the elements of the unconscious is achieved through bringing this material into the conscious mind.

The Development of Psychoanalysis

The idea of psychoanalysis was first started to receive serious attention and definite shape under Sigmund Freud, a neurologist trying to find an effective treatment for patients with neurotic or hysterical symptoms, who formulated his own theory of psychoanalysis in Vienna in the 1890s. When Freud was employed as a neurological consultant at the Children's Hospital, he realised that there were mental processes that were not conscious as he noticed that many aphasic children had no apparent organic cause for their symptoms. He then wrote a monograph about the subject. In 1885, Freud obtained a grant to study with Jean-Martin Charcot, a famed neurologist in Paris, where Freud followed the clinical presentations of Charcot, particularly in the areas of hysteria, paralyses and the anaesthesis.

Freud's first theory to explain hysterical symptoms was presented in Studies on Hysteria (1895), co-authored with his mentor, the distinguished physician, Josef Breuer, which was generally considered as the birth of psychoanalysis. The work was based on Breuer's treatment of Bertha Pappenheim, referred to in case studies by the pseudonym "Anna O", where Freud contended that at the root of hysterical symptoms were repressed memories of distressing occurrences, almost due to direct or indirect sexual associations.

Freud's seduction theory proposed that the preconditions for hysterical symptoms are sexual excitations in infancy, and he claimed to have uncovered repressed memories of incidents of sexual abuse for all his patients. The theory emphasises the causative impact of nurture and the shaping of the mind by experience. It also held that hysteria and obsession neurosis are caused by repressed memories of infantile sexual abuse. The theory stated that Infant sexual abuse was the root of all neurosis and is the major cause for premature introduction of sexuality into the experience of the child.

Topographic theory was named and first described by Sigmund Freud in *The Interpretation of Dreams* (1900). The theory formulates that the mental apparatus can be divided into the systems Conscious, Preconscious, and Unconscious and these systems are not anatomical structures of the brain but mental processes. Although Freud retained this theory throughout his life, he largely replaced it with the Structural theory The Topographic theory remains as one of the meta-psychological points of view for describing how the mind functions in classical psychoanalytic theory. By 1900, Freud had theorised that dreams had symbolic significance and were specific to the dreamer. Freud formulated his second psychological theory which hypotheses that the unconscious has or is a "primary process" consisting of symbolic and condensed thoughts, and a "secondary process" of logical, conscious thoughts. This theory was published in 1900, *The Interpretation of Dreams.* Chapter VII whereFreud used the analogy of an iceberg to describe the three levels of the mind.

In 1905, Freud published *Three Essays on the Theory of Sexuality* in which he laid out his discovery of psychosexual phases. His early formulation included the idea that because of societal restrictions, sexual wishes were repressed into an unconscious state, and that the energy of these unconscious wishes could be turned into anxiety or physical symptoms. Therefore, the early treatment techniques, including hypnotism and abreaction, were designed to make the unconscious conscious in order to relieve the pressure and the apparently resulting symptoms.

Freud summarised the ideas of id, ego, and superego in a book entitled, *The Ego and the Id.* In the book, he revised the whole theory of mental functioning that repression was only one of many defense mechanisms, and that it occurred to reduce anxiety. Hence, Freud characterised repression as both the cause and result of anxiety. In 1926, in *Inhibitions, Symptoms and Anxiety,* Freud characterised how intra- psychic conflict among drive and superego caused anxiety, and how that anxiety lead to an inhibition of mental functions, such as intellect and speech. Freud later developed a more structural model of the mind comprising the entities id, ego and superego which are referred by Freud as "the psychic apparatus" and are the hypothetical conceptualisations of important mental functions. Freud had also conceptualized that ego can deploy various defense mechanisms to prevent it from becoming overwhelmed by anxiety.

Psychoanalysis is a widely known theory not only for its concepts but also for its interest incited by its theraupatical method. The therapy has also the virtues of its application to other domains such as literature, sociology, anthropology, ethnology, religion and mythology inciting the interest of public that had no inclination towards the clinical realm. It also distinguished itself through media using the most common means: radio, TV or film scripts. There was even a movie dedicated to Sigmund Freud which presented the incertitude years of his beginnings in psychoanalysis.

It is evident that the predominant psychoanalytic theories is organised into several theoretical schools which although differ in their basic ideals, most of them emphasise the influence of unconscious elements on the conscious. In the field of psychoanalysis, there are persistent conflicts regarding specific causes and disputes regarding the ideal treatment techniques. In the 21st century, psychoanalytic ideas are embedded in Western culture especially in the field of children, education, literary criticism, cultural studies, mental health, psychotherapy etc. There is a mainstream of evolved analytic ideas but also there are groups who follow the precepts of one or more of the later theoreticians. The outline of the predominant schools of psychoanalysis is given below:

The Different Schools Rooted from Psychoanalysis

Freud between 1895 and 1905 developed a burst of creative thinking and innovative clinical techniques. His theories were always inspired and stimulated in Freud's clinical efforts which undoubtedly stimulated more theoretical advances. In the decade, psychoanalysis emerged from hypnotism and became a distinct methodology and treatment in its own and also the basic concepts that guide psychoanalytic thoughts to the present day were established. Stephen A Mitchell and Margaret J Black remarks:

The site of Freud's dig was not the earth but the mind of his patients; the tools he used were not a shovel and brush but psychoanalytic interpretations. The exhilaration was the same, however, Freud felt he had designed an important site and had fashioned the necessary technology for exposing the underlying structure of the human mind and for unearthing the archaic history of both the individual patient and all humankind. (1)

Ego Psychology

Ego psychology was originated from Sigmund Freud's id-ego-superego model. Freud's functionalist version of the ego was further elaborated by a number of prominent psychoanalytic theorists like Hartmann, Loewenstein, and Kris in a series of papers and books from 1939 through the late 1960s, theorising the various functions of ego and how they can be impaired in psychopathology. Their major concern was around strengthening the ego which could cope with the pressures of the id, super-ego, and society in general as the central functions of the ego were reality-testing, impulse-control, judgment, defense and synthetic functioning.

According to ego psychology, ego strengths include the capacities to control oral, sexual, and destructive impulses; to tolerate painful effects; and to prevent the eruption into consciousness of symbolic fantasy. Synthetic functions arise from the development of the ego and serve the purpose of managing the conflict processes and so to protect the conscious mind from its awareness of forbidden impulses and thoughts. One of the main purposes of ego psychology is to emphasise that mental functions are not derivatives of wishes, affects, or defenses. However, unconscious conflicts can affect secondarily the autonomous ego functions

Modern Conflict Theory

The objective of modern conflict-theory psychoanalysis is to change the balance of conflict in a patient by making aspects of the less adaptive solutions conscious to be rethought and hence more adaptive solutions can be found.The theory is a revised version of structural theory and a variation of ego psychology which is most notably significant and different by altering concepts related to where repressed thoughts were stored and also centers on how emotional symptoms and traits are complex solutions to mental conflict. The theory posits the conscious and unconscious conflicts, whereas dispenses with the concepts of a fixed id, ego and superegoamong wishes, emotions and defensive operations that are shut off from consciousness. The healthy functioning is also determined by resolutions of conflicts.

Object Relations Theory

Object relations theory emphasises interpersonal relations in the family, especially between mother and child. "Object" means person, that is, the object or target of another's feelings or intentions. The theory holds that the infant's experience in relationship with the mother is the primary determinant of personality formation and the child's need for attachment is the motivating factor in the development of the infantile self. "Relations" refers to the interpersonal relations and suggests the remainders of past relationships that affect a person in the present. The theory is the resultant of the work of British analysts Ronald Fairbairn, Donald Winnicott, and others of the British Independent group, augmented by that of Melanie Klein and the Kleinian groups. Object relations theorists are interested in inner images of the self and how they manifest themselves in interpersonal situations through a study of how internal representations of the self and others are organized. The clinical symptoms that suggest object relations problems include disturbances in an individual's capacity to feel warmth, empathy, identity stability, consistent emotional closeness, and stability in relationships with significant others. Concepts regarding internal representations although often attributed to Melanie Klein, were first mentioned by Sigmund Freud in his early concepts of drive theory.

Jacques Lacan and Lacanian Psychoanalysis

Lacanian psychoanalysis maintains a distinctive position in relation to other forms of therapeutic enquiry for it marks a return to Freud. Lacania psychoanalysis integrates psychoanalysis with structural linguistics and Hegelian philosophy, is popular in France and parts of Latin America. The theory is a departure from the traditional British and American psychoanalysis, which is predominantly Ego psychology. Jacques Lacan claimed that his theories were an extension of Freud's own and also claims the necessity of reading Freud's complete works, not only a part of them. Lacan's concepts concern and claim that the unconscious is structured as a language. In spite of a great influence on psychoanalysis in France and parts of Latin America, Lacan and his ideas have taken longer to be translated into English and so had a lesser impact on psychoanalysis and psychotherapy in the UK and the US. Hence his ideas are most widely used to analyze texts in literary theory.

Interpersonal Psychoanalysis

Interpersonal psychoanalysis theory was first introduced by Harry Stack Sullivan, MD, and developed further by Frieda Fromm-Reichmann, Clara Thompson, Erich Fromm, and others who contributed to the founding of the William Alanson White Institute and Interpersonal Psychoanalysis in general. The theory accents the nuances of interpersonal interactions, especially how individuals protect themselves from anxiety by establishing collusive interactions with others, and the relevance of actual experiences with other persons. The therapy utilizes a uniquely structured model for the treatment of mental health issues which are based on attachment and communication theories, Interpersonal psychotherapy was initially developed as a brief therapy for depression as people with depressive symptoms often experience problems in their interpersonal relationships, In general, interpersonal therapists provide active, non-judgmental treatment in order to help people in therapy successfully handle challenges and improve mental health.

Feminist Psychoanalysis

Feminist theories of psychoanalysis emerged towards the second half of the 20th century to articulate the feminine subjects like sexual differences and the mode of development from the point of view of female. According to Freud, male is a subject and female is an object. For Freud the mother is structured as the object of the infant's rejection and destruction. For Lacan, the "woman" can either receive the phallic symbolic as an object or embody a lack in the symbolic facet that informs the structure of the human subject. Feminist psychoanalysis is mostly post-Freudian and post-Lacanian with theorists likeToril Moi, Joan Copjec, Juliet Mitchell, Teresa Brennan and Griselda Pollock. Feminist psychoanalysts review Art and Mythology following French feminist psychoanalysis, the gaze and sexual difference in the case of woman where they answer and comment the question of the feminine and love, informs and includes gender, queer and post-feminist theories.

Modern Psychoanalysis

Modern psychoanalysis is a term coined by Hyman Spotnitz and his colleagues to describe a body of theoretical and clinical approaches that aim to extend Freud's theories. Itis based on the clinical approach and theoretical framework of Sigmund Freud, who defined psychoanalysis as any line of study and investigation that takes transference and resistance as the initial point of its work. The theory is also applicable to the full range of emotional disorders including neuroses, psychoses, borderline conditions, depression, and character disorders and widens the potential for treatment that are considered to be untreatable by classical approaches.Interventions based on this approach intend to provide an emotional communication to the patient, rather than to promote intellectual insight. These interventions are used to resolve resistances that are present in the clinical setting. This school of psychoanalysis has nurtured training opportunities for students in the United States and from countries worldwide and also in their journals where Modern Psychoanalysis has been published since 1976. As a whole, the findings of modern psychoanalysis have contributed new insights into the dynamics of emotional illnesses and the mechanisms through which the analytic process cures these conditions.

Introduction to Self Psychology

Self Psychology is a modern psychoanalytic theory introduced by Heinz Kohut in the 1960s, 70s, and 80s, and is developing as a contemporary form of psychoanalytic treatment. The theory was introduced in the early 70's with the publication of Heinz Kohut's famous monograph,, *The Analysis of the Self*. Self Psychology has enhanced into the most significant analytic theory since Freud first introduced psychoanalysis in the early 20th century. The theory provides the basis for most of the therapeutic benefits of the contemporary psychoanalysis. While rejecting the primary importance of innate Freudian sexual drives in the organization of the human psyche, Self Psychology was the first major psychoanalytic movement in the United States to recognize the critical and significant role of empathy in explaining human development and psychoanalytic changes. The effort is made to understand individuals from within their subjective experience on the understanding of the self as the central agency of the human psyche. Self Psychology is also considered as a major break from traditional psychoanalysis and as the beginnings of the relational approach to psychoanalysis. Neil J Skolnick and Susan C Warshaw portrays:

Self Psychology holds that self- selfobject relationships from the essence of psychological life from birth to death, that a move from dependence (symbiosis) to independence (autonomy) in the psychological sphere is no more possible, let alone desirable, than a corresponding move from a life dependent on oxygen to a life independent of it in the biological sphere. (47)

Heinz Kohut's contribution to psychology is an established and embedded one. He postulated his view of the self with four basic components, beginning with the nuclear self which is the biological construct that infants are born with. The virtual self is an outcome of the baby retained by the parents. The grouping of the nuclear self and the virtual self leads to the emergence of a cohesive self. On the other hand, trauma, abuse, and other problems during the development of a child can prevent the normal development of the cohesive self. The grandiose self is the fourth component which is an egocentric form of the self that results from feelings of being the center of the universe during early childhood.

Heinz Kohut believed that a parent's failure to empathise with the child was nearly the basic reason behind every psychological problem. The theory of Self Psychology emphasises that psychological problems are the result of unmet developmental needs of a child. Empathy is the most important therapeutic tool in Self Psychology as according to Kohut it would help to recover the damages caused by unmet developmental needs of an individual in his early childhood. Heinz Kohut comments that empathy has healing effects which can also be used as an intellectual tool that wins the client's trust allowing the therapist to gain more useful information in order to develop effective therapeutic strategies. This theory of Self Psychology is applied and analysed in the select novels of Arun Joshi and Kiran Desai demonstrating the reasons for the disorder of self and the process and development of the cohesive self,

Indian English Literature

To illustrate further the biography, bibliography, contemporary writers, the style of writing and the achievements of Arun Joshi and Kiran Desai areexpounded. To begin with Indian writing in English is one of the voices in which India speaks. C.R. Reddy has pointed out in his foreword to K.R. Srinivasa Iyengar's P.E.N book that:

Indo Anglian literature is not essentially different in kind from Indian literature. It is a part of it, a modern facet of that glory which, commencing from the Vedas, has continued to spread its mellow light now with greater and now with lesser brilliance under the inexorable vicissitude, of time and history. (3)

Thus Indians aspiring to accomplish creative self-expression through the medium of English language has given rise to Indian writings in English. Indian fiction in English like other branches of Indo-English literature, originated and grew up under the tutelage of the English men The first Indian novel in English is Bankim Chandra Chatterjee's, *Rajmohan's Wife* which appeared in 1864.

Indo- English fiction in its earlier stage involved itself with the history of India. The exposure to western thinking and the spread of English education led to the East-West comparisons which contrasted the traditional Indian norms. There were historical romances of the nineteenth and the early twentieth century. Few examples are S K Nikambe's *Ratnabai* (1895), R C Dutts *The Slave Girl of Agra* (1909), S K Goshs *The Prince of Destiny* and S K Mitra's *The Hindupur* (1909). Then in the 1930's and 1940's emerged a new trend in the Indian-English novels which exhibited the social and political realism that existed where the authors took up the contemporary social and political problems. The novelists of this period were inspired and influenced by the freedom movement of Mahathma Gandhi which gave base to novels like K S Venkatramani's *Murugan the Tiller* (1927) and *Kandan, the Patriot* (1932).

The influence of freedom movement continued in Indian- English writing even after the Independence and it reflected in the novels of R K Narayan, K A Abbas, N Nagarajan, Raja Rao, Manohar Malgaonkar, Nayantara Sahgal and Chaman Nahal. Also the entire Indian – English writings can be divided into two parts. They are those of Pre Independence period and Post Independence period. Novels in the Pre Independence period became a very powerful medium for the propagation of patriotic sentiments. The Pre Independence period includes the writings of Mulk Raj Anand, Raja Rao, R.K. Narayan, who are rightly described as the Big three. William Walsh aptly writes "It was those three who defined the area in which the Indian novel was to operate. They established the suppositions, the manner, the idiom, the concept of character and the nature of the themes which were to give the Indian novel its particular distinctiveness."(2).

These novelists reveal the social, economic and political realities of India. Mulk Raj Anand is the first Indian writer to give Indian- English novel a definite tone and texture. In his *Untouchable* (1935), *Coolie* (1936) and *Two Leaves and a Bud* (1937). He takes a humanitarian stance for the depressed and suppressed. R K Narayan, the distinguished writer, explored the South Indian middle class milleu in his Malgudi fiction: *Swami and Friends* (1935), *The Bachelor of Arts*(1937), *The Dark Room*(1938), and *The English Teacher*(1946). His *Vendor of Sweets* and *The Man- Eater of Malgudi* (1962) present the clashing and coalescing of the traditional and the traditional values.

The traditional social realism by Mulk Raj Anand was followed by novelists like Kamala Markandaya, Bhabani Bhattacharya, Kushwant Singh and Chaman Nahal. The Post Independence writers like Kamala Markandaya, Arun Joshi, Ruth Prawer Jhabvala and Anita Desai voice forth the human predicament through the negative social forces that subvert man's progress.

Arun Joshi is an eminent writer in the pre-Rushdie era. He wrote at a time when Indian fiction in English had not gained reputation in the West and its chances of success were also poor at home. His novels are serious and powerfully disturbing. In his novels, Arun Joshi skillfully brings out the aspects of Indian life where he demonstrates the rapid Westernization of life in India. Arun Joshi, in his novels, attempts a serious probe into the existential problems and disturbances of mankind by focusing on certain individualistic characters. He shined as a novelist of outstaying repute in the circle of Indian scholars and critics. His literary career followed an ascending line which ultimately led him to win India's most prestigious literary prize the Sahitya Academy Award.

Arun Joshi was a son of a famous botanist and eminent academician.

Arun Joshi was born as the youngest child of his parents at Benares on July 7, 1939. He lived in Benares till he was seven. He spent the rest of his childhood in Lahore and then moved to Indian Punjab during the tragic events of partition. He was a brilliant student and was sent to the U.S.A. to pursue his higher education where he studied at various centers of education. He obtained a degree in Engineering and Industrial Management from the University of Kansas in 1959 and Master's from M.I.T. Arun Joshi's stay in the U.S.A., remained an influential factor in his life. Joshi's interests and passions were aroused not by the field, but rather by a totally unrelated one, psychiatry. He worked in a mental hospital where he met with chronic schizophrenics. It is an experience which left deep impression on him. Joshi went back to India where he started his career as the management staff of an Indian Company. He joined D.C.M. in 1961 as chief of its recruitment and training department. In 1964, he married Rukmani Lal, the daughter of a D.C.M. share holder and subsequently held many positions in the company. His association with the D.C.M. as an important executive, prompted him to attempt a domestic biography in 1975 of *Lala Sri Ram; A study in Entrepreneurship in Industrial Management.*In 1965, he resigned from the D.C.M. but continued to be the Executive Director of Sri Ram Centre for Industrial Relations and Human Resources, and he had his own separate industrial establishments to manufacture diesel engines. Thus, Arun Joshi who was a dynamic industrialist was at the same time an outstanding novelist.

In the modern world, man aspires and run after something or other. He lives his life more like a machine where he follows a routine order of purposeless life. One of the problems that modern man suffer is that his oscillation between to be a person of self or to be a person dominated by other external forces. Both the extremes bring tremendous problems in the lives of human beings. This concept is highlighted in the novels of Arun Joshi. R.S. Singh comments that in Arun Joshi's novels "There is struggle in man's heart himself. He cannot decide what to do; whether one should confess one's guilt or not, whether one should reconcile with evil spirits or go hand in hand with one's soul" (115).

Arun Joshi's fictional works are products of the various influences upon his mind and art. He was influenced by the writers and philosophers from both East and West. Though his profession was related to management, his avocation from the very beginning had been in writing. He was highly influenced by the works which were available in English translations, especially those of the French novelists such as Sartre and Camus.

In his contribution to *The Fictional World of Arun Joshi* (1986) edited by R.K. Dhawan, Joshi poses the questions and replies to them by quoting the lines of Freud. The questions are "From time to time, I am asked why I write? Why I pick the themes that I pick and why I treat them in the manners that I do?" The answer that he quotes is:

There is, in fact, a path from phantasy back again to reality, and that is art. The artist has also an introverted disposition and has not far to go to become neurotic... He longs to attain, honour, power, riches, fame and the love of women; but he lacks the means of achieving these gratifications. So, like any other with an unsatisfied longing, he turns away from reality and transfers all his interests and all his libido to, onto the creation of his wishes in the life of Phantasy. (85)

It becomes clear that phantasy and reality are important to Arun Joshi where the concepts of phantasy are realized through reality and the reality materializes phantasy. This factor of Freud had a deep influence upon Arun Joshi's fiction. In the words of Hari Mohan Prasad, Joshi is "a novelist in the tradition of Kafka, Camus, Sartre and Saul Bellow, Elison and Malamud" (10). Some of the contemporary writers of Arun Joshi are Kamala Markandaya, Ruth Prawer Jhabvala, Nayantara Sahgal, Anita Desai, Manohar Malgonkar, Chaman Nahal.

Arun Joshi's output in the genre of fiction is limited to five novels such as *The Foreigner* (1968), *The Strange Case of Billy Biswas* (1971), *The Apprentice* (1974*)*, *The Last Labyrinth* (1981) and *The City and the River* (1990) along *The Survivor* (1975), a book of collection of his ten short stories. Besides the ten short stories two other stories are published in magazine. There is also a work of biography entitled *Lala Sri Ram; A study in Entrepreneurship in Industrial management* (1975).

The themes of Arun Joshi novels are full of tension, struggle and conflicts. There are fathers who are dissatisfied with the children and children with their parents. For instance in *The strange case of Billy Biswas,* Billy studies anthropology, while his father thinks that his son is pursuing engineering in a Western university. Mr. Biswas becomes angry when he comes to know that Billy has done Ph.D in Anthropology. Secondly, there is a clash between husband and wife. In *TheLast Labyrinth,* Som Bhaskar is totally neutral to his wife, Geeta. While *The Apprentice,* Ratna Rathor is tired of his wife.

Apart from these themes, there is a struggle in man's heart. He is unable to decide what to do, whether to reconcile with evil and external spirits or go hand in hand with one's soul or self. R.K. Pathak has remarked:

Arun Joshi is one of those modern Indian novelists in English who have broken new grounds. In search of new themes, he has 'renounced the larger world in favour of the inner man' and has engaged himself in 'a search for the essence of human living'. An outstanding novelist of human predicament, Joshi has chartered in all his four novels the inner crisis of the modern man. (45)

The novels of Arun Joshi are not pessimistic in its temper. It brings out man's capacity to endure hardship. He becomes refined enduring those hardships. For example, Sindi Oberoi becomes the bread-giver to the factory men. Nature is a prominent factor in Joshi's novels. It is presented in its various aspects and its sensuous presentations are very colourful and charming.

The social evils like lying, hypocrisy, bribery, drunkenness, woman-izing and unfair distribution of money are brought to limelight in Joshi's novels. Joshi has also highlighted the various problems in the course of his novels like the problem of unemployment, population explosion, etc. Arun Joshi's characters are based on reality and the author lets them grow naturally. The characters suffer from a deep sense of depression, frustration and alienation, but they eventually emerge triumphant. In the case of Billy Biswas, his death must be considered only as the triumph of his ideals.

The contemporary Indian English writing has been acknowledged and renowned all over the world as the writers have created their new paths and got rewards for their works in English where the Indo-English fiction has undergone a complete transformation from its traditional norms which involved itself with the history of India. Later the exposure to western thinking led to the East-West comparisons which contrasted the traditional Indian norms. As a result there were eminent writers pro-jecting their creative talents both during the Pre Independence and Post Independence period. In the late twentieth-century writers like Arun-thathi Roy, Salman Rushdie and writers of Indian origin are recognized globally who compete the native writers and have received the presti-gious awards for Literature. The one who had also enlisted her name in this list is Kiran Desai, a promising Indian writer in English born in 1971 in India and the daughter of the renowned Indian English novelist, Anita Desai. Kiran Desai was educated in India, England and the United States. Her first novel, *Hullabaloo in the Guava Orchard*, was written in the year 1998 and it was remarked by Salman Rushdie as lush and intensely imagined. The Times has also commented that Kiran Desai is the most appealing voice of the new generation and also her book is fresh, funny and delicious which defies comparison with that of any other novelist.

The novel has won the 1998 Betty Trask Prize, serialized in The New Yorker and included in the Vintage Book of Indian Writing. Kiran Desai's second novel, *The Inheritance of Loss*, won the Man Booker Prize in the year 2006 and was shortlisted for the Orange Broadband Prize for Fiction in the year 2007. The judges called the novel as a magnificent novel of human breath and wisdom, comic tenderness and powerful political acuteness. Thus Kiran Desai is a well-recognized novelist all over the world.

Hullabaloo in the Guava Orchard is about a protagonist who climbs a tree in order to withdraw himself from his mundane life in search of peace. He stays there, revered as a saint by the people and the story is about the problems that he faces because of his family and people, and eventually his end. Ankita Shukla and Anshul Chandra comment that the novel brings to light the different nature of the character from that of others. They comment the novel and its idea which "describes man's craving to escape from his 'real' world to his imagined world of freedom, peace, space and solace". When asked by an interviewer about the genesis of Hullabaloo in the Guava Orchard, Kiran Desai said that she "started with a very small idea" (6).It is possible that in writing *The Inheritance of Loss* Kiran Desai started with much big and better idea about India in its post- colonial condition and multicultural diversity.

Kiran Desai's second novel *The Inheritance of Loss*, was published in 2006 and was heralded all over the world and she became the youngest woman writer to have ever received the fifty thousand pound award. It was a career stirring event for a budding novelist and particularly an honour that has eluded her celebrated mother, Anita Desai, who has been a finalist thrice for the prize. In this novel, Kiran Desai highlights the current global issues such as globalization, inequality, multiculturalism, racism, immigrant issues etc.

Kiran Desai is a conscious craftsman who builds up her plot skillfully and she has the ability to tell the story artistically. Her work exhibits a stretched action line and displays the spectacle of life with a gallery of characters. Her vast and colourful imagination gives richness and a feel of magic to her novels coated with sensitiveness and humour. Also in her novels, the mundane background of the characters is transformed to something unique, projecting their own identity by Kiran Desai's imagination and rich humour.

The concept of the development of cohesive self as postulated by Heinz Kohut in his Self Psychology is analysed on the protagonists based on their situation, crisis and trauma faced by them in the novels of Arun Joshi and KIran Desai. Heinz Kohut had enlisted the aspects of self as:

- our sense of being an independent center of initiative and perception,

- of being integrated with our most central ambitions and ideals,

- and with our experience that our body and mind form a unit in space and a continuum intime. (155)

These features of the self are given breath and life only with the mother's empathic care for the child's entire self, by which Heinz Kohut means an atmosphere of acceptance. The developing grandiose self of a child is reflected in the radiance of the mother as its own grandiosity shares in the omnipotence of its first selfobject. The child's selfobjects reacts to its utterances as if it already had a self, or a self-experience of its own initiative, integrity and continuity. It impliesthat if empathic care by the mother is to be successful, she should not only take care of the infant's requirements and achievements but also speaks to the child as an integral whole. Hence Kohut uses the self-selfobject relationship to designate this state of affairs where selfobjects are objects or functions of objects which stimulate the self-feeling, maintain it, or influence it positively. Kohut remarks:

The selfobject which possesses a mature psychological organization able to realistically evaluate the child's needs and how to meet them will be absorbed by the child into its own psychological organization and rectify the child's homeostatic disequilibrium through behavior. (9)

For Kohut, the child's earliest expressions of narcissistic rageand anxiety are indications of a rudimentary self. In the early stage, the parents will supportively mirror the strivings of the child's grandiose self and not threaten their idealization as parents. When the nuclear self has established itself, a stronger movement toward disillusionment begins. The nuclear self consists of strivings (ambitions) which spring from the grandiose self and transform ideals, goals, and values from the idealized parent imago. The tension arc between these poles mobilises talents and acquired abilities which serves as the "abiding flow of actual psychological activity ... between the two poles of the self" and of a tension gradient, an "action-producing state which arises between man's strivings and his ideals" (157). Kohut defines the self, its features and function as:

The self (within the framework of self psychology in the narrow sense, one must now add) emerges in the psychoanalytic situation and is conceptualized, in the mode of a comparatively low level, i.e., comparatively experience- near, psychoanalytic abstraction, as a content of the mental apparatus...it is a structure within the mind...it has continuity in time, i.e., it is enduring...the self has, furthermore, also a psychic location.... The, then, quite analogous to the representations of objects, is a content of the mental apparatus but is not one of its constituents, i.e., not one of the agencies of mind. (450, 451)

The quality of the interactions between the self and its selfobjects in childhood, decide the self as a firm and healthy structure or as a more or less seriously damaged one. As a result, the adult self exists in conditions of varying degrees of coherence, from cohesion to fragmentation and also in varying degrees of functional harmony, from order to chaos. The disorder in self is due to the failure to achieve cohesion, vigour, or harmony. In such case, the damaged self strives to achieve a state of cohesion and inner harmony. According to Kohut difficulties in the development of self along the grandiosity, idealization, and connectedness dimensions lead to disorders of the self, which leads to the lack of self-cohesion, confidence and susceptible self-esteem. When the self has crystallized, it aims towards the understanding of its own specific programme of action that is determined by its constituent ambitions, goals, skills and talents, and also because of the pressures that arise between these constituents. In self psychology, cohesive self-structure is the outcome of normal healthy development along the grandiosity, idealization, and connectedness dimensions. In other words, self-cohesion is attained when individuals posses ambitions,ideals, and values.The acceptability of one's personality, talents, and skills contributes to a cohesive self-structure which results in a sense of stability, and permanence.

Hypothesis

The self is one of the most heavily researched areas in social and personality psychology. Whatever stance one adopts regarding the self, it depends on the many phenomena of which the self is a predicate—self-knowledge, self-awareness, self-esteem, self-enhancement, self-regulation, self-deception, self-presentation are major research areas. Also the study of the self extends far beyond the topics that explicitly orient the term. Social comparison theory comprises studies on how people define their characteristics by assessing where they stand relative to others. Hence the study of the self extends beyond psychology: philosophers, anthropologists, sociologists, fiction writers and other artists are fascinated with the self. The major topics related to self-functioning that social and personality psychologists address concern the ways in which people understand and define their characteristics, how people use task and social feedback to monitor their progress, the influence of individual standards, prospects, and values on perception of others, and how people maintain desired self-images. Hence the self has been studied as an individual difference variable, a determinant of social cognizance, attribution, and judgment, and as an indispensable element in social relations. Hence the study is to bring out the reason behind the disorder self due to the disturbances and the process and development of a cohesive self based on the Self psychology theory postulated by Heinz Kohut and developed by his followers. In general literary studies are examined on topics related to self and the psychological conflicts. But there are only rare indepth studies on the reason behind the loss of self and psychological conflicts in a character which lead to trauma, loss of happiness and purposein life. This study is a step ahead on analyzing the reason behind the lack of self and the steps to develop a cohesive self of maintaining a mutual understanding with others. The best part of the study is that the comparative analysis of the works of Arun Joshi and Kiran Desai can be applied to mankind ingeneral where they lack self in search of peace and happiness in life. Thus the study explores the way to nurture the self with concrete ideas in order to live a life of satisfaction of use to others.

Aim and Objective of the Research

1. a) To highlight the importance of self in an individual based on the theory of Self Psychology.
2. b) To present the self as a psychological power influencing healthy personality and also personality disorder.
3. c) To throw light on the importance of selfobject needs like mirroring, merging and idealisation for the development of the cohesive self.
4. d) To illustrate both Billy Biswas of *The Strange Case of Billy Biswas* and Sampath of *Hullabaloo in the Guava Orchard* as typical examples of protagonists who possess disorder self due to the

lack of the interplay between them and their parents in their early childhood.

5. e) To trace the process of development of the cohesive self in spite of the disturbances as depicted through the protagonists,Ratan of *The Apprentice* and Jemubhai of *The Inheritance of Loss.*

6. f) To summate the application of Self Psychology as a good therapy to treat narcissistic behaviour and narcissistic personality disorder.

Review of Literature

Although a great deal of research on the psychology of self can be surveyed on the nature of selfhood dates back to pre-scientific philosophy first published in 1641 is a testament not only to the theoretical intrigue of the self as a construct of study to the current understanding of self and identity.. Leary and Tangney 2012 offers the most authoritative compilation of contemporary scholarship on selfhood, while Baumeister 1999 provides a collection of some of the most influential empirical works to advance the scientific study of self. Brown 1998 and Sedikides and Spencer 2007 provide broad overviews of the field's extant understanding of self, with the former aimed at undergraduate audiences and the latter toward graduate students and beyond. Baumeister 1998 is a chapter in the *Handbook of Social Psychology* that offers a systematic, comprehensive survey of historical and contemporary research on the self, and Fiske 2004 emphasises the inherently social nature of the manifestations of selfhood. Finally, Kruglanski, et al. 1996, a special issue of *Journal of Personality and Social Psychology*, presents a unifying collection of research that demonstrates the necessarily interdisciplinary nature of self and identity.

In the case of works on Self Psychology, Heinz Kohut had himself published a number of books which furnish his ideas and concepts that formed the basis of modern psychoanalysis. His publicatins are *The Analysis of the Self: A Systematic Approach to the Psychoanalytic Treatment of Narcissistic Personality Disorders (1971), The Restoration of the Self (1977), The Search for the Self, Selected Writings of Heinz Kohut 1950–1978, Volume 1 and Volume II (1978)*edited by Paul Ornstein.*The Psychology of the Self: A Casebook*is published in collaboration with Arnold Goldberg. Few of his works were published posthumously. They are*How Does Analysis Cure?* (1984), *Self Psychology and the Humanities* (1985), *The Kohut Seminars on Self Psychology and Psychotherapy With Adolescents and Young Adults* (1987), *The Search for the Self: Selected Writings of Heinz Kohut: 1978–1981. Vol. 3.* (1990) and Volume 4 (1991), *The Curve of Life: Correspondence of Heinz Kohut, 1923–1981* (1994), *The Chicago Institute Lectures* (1996). Also there are number of books and research articles substantiating and developing the ideas of Heinz Kohut.

The essence of Kohut's contribution to psychoanalysis is that he found a theory to retain a depth psychology that places a different and innovative emphasis on empathy and so enhances the direct and symbolic involvement of the self in the world. Kohut altered the ideas about narcissism, about aggression and rage, about dreams, about the relationship between psychoanalysis and the humanities in general. As a result there is a change in many of the ethical values and ultimately the very meaning of the self in human experience. These characteristics make Self psychology influence various genre, for instance, there are research papers related to music, philosophy, literary text etc. The paper "Word and Music" by Frank M lachmann is based on music, whereas "The Life of the Soul, An Essay in Ecological Thinking" by John H Riker is related to philosophy. Self Psychology and its concepts are applied in literary texts, for instance, "Chivolry, 'Mutiny', and Sherlock Holmes: Three Aspects of

Imperial Grandiosity and Rage" by Dianne Simmons, "Toni Morrison's Beloved, The Empathic Connection and the Restoration of the Self" by Elizabeth O Brien. The present study is a comparative analysis based on the theory of Self Psychology which demonstratrs the reason for the disorder in self and the development of cohesive self by providing an overview of Kohut's Self Psychology, its salient features and concepts.

2

Self Psychology Theory and Theorists

If there is one lesson that I have learned during my life as an analyst, it is the lesson that what my patients tell me is likely to be true - that many times when I believed that I was right and my patients were wrong, it turned out, though often only after a prolonged search, that my rightness was superficial whereas their rightness was profound.

Heinz Kohut

This chapter explores Self Psychology developed by Heinz Kohut which is widely accepted as one of the central psychoanalytic theories. Self Psychology has been further developed by Arnold Goldberg, Frank M Lachmann, Paul and Anna Ornstein, Marian Tolpin, and others. Kohut viewed the self as a psychological power that explains the development of an established and healthy personality as well as the formation of personality disorders. The theory also emphasises the development of amalgamated sense of self through empathic contacts with other individuals, the primary important others considered as selfobjects that meet the developing self's needs for mirroring, idealization, and twinship, and thus strengthen the developing self. The process of treatment is done through "transmuting internalizations" in which the patient gradually internalises the selfobject functions provided by the therapist. Kohut stated that Self psychology is "at one with the technical principle that interpretation in general, and the interpretation of transferences in particular, is the major instrumentality of therapeutic psychoanalysis" (210).

During the 1970s, Kohut's theory of Self Psychology gained popularity rapidly. Many people who struggled with guilt resulting from material indulgence and the self-serving behaviours regarded Self psychology as a more positive and understanding approach to therapy than traditional psychoanalysis. Because of its accepting approach, Self Psychology has become one of the foundations of modern psychology, along with object relation theory, ego psychology, and the theory of drive and motivation.

Kohut's Self Psychology constitutes a tremendous leap in the depth psychology movement. Kohut attempted to understand what was going on in the life of a client and capture this in a more nuanced way than theoreticians. In contrast to the traditional psychoanalytical theory, Kohut consciously ends up with a model that could better explain observed behaviour of a client. The phenomena of mirroring, selfobject idealization, merging and optimal frustration are concepts that offer a standard by which to judge healthy and unhealthy development of the self. Additionally, Kohut's understanding of narcissistically-based behavior as an attempt to get unmet developmental needs by seeking an ideal selfobject who will mirror the client seems more efficacious in treatment than the more traditional understanding of narcissism. Also Kohut's model is relevant to the understanding and treatment of addiction which can be viewed as a particularly extreme outcome of the failures in developmental processes.

In his initial stage, Kohut did little to distinguish himself besides playing expertly by the rules. For many years he was a highly orthodox professional who was studious about the advancement of his career reflecting other senior figures in the analytical world. Kohut came out with his first book, or found the force of his originality only when he reached his 50's, as Strozier's comments that it is a curious fact of Kohut's creativity as his major theoretical work came in the second half of his sixth decade.

Kohut's *The Analysis of the Self* was published in 1971 which represents the image of the narcissistic ego which Freud put forward in 1914 and explores its multiple implications. Kohut argues that children tend to begin their life with fantasies ofthe grandiose self and ideal parents.But when the child develops these illusions that they framed are tamed and combined into a mature personality. Grandiosity is repressed in such case which leads to self-esteem where the idealization of the parent becomes the basis for a child's strongest morals and values. In the case of trauma in a person's early childhood, the version of the self remains unchanged which lead to an unhealthy psyche. Also the grandiose self is inactive which ultimately results in what Kohut famously termed as Narcissistic Personality Disorder.

Kohut believed that he was reshaping psychoanalysis to respond to the nature in which he found himself as in the midcentury in America, the self was the central botheration and narcissism was the central drawback for which the mode of analysts had to be reset. Heunderstands narcissism as the poor object relations to selfobjects and the healthy development of self will entail the transformation of most selfobjects into mental structures so that they function to a certain extent independently on their original external ground. St. Clair explains that healthy development entails the child coming to see the selfobject as separate, while idealized aspects of the selfobject are interjected as the superego. If an individual gets stuck at the childhood stage of irritabilities and the self remains largely un-mirrored and un-integrated with the rest of the developing self, his behaviour is likely to become increasingly pathological. Narcissism for Kohut is not to be understood, as Freud did, in terms of drives and conflicts, but as the result of a breakdown in the child's relation to a selfobject. In particular, narcissism results from a failure of caregivers to adequately fulfill the functions discussed earlier, whereas Freud viewed narcissism simply as a worse thing. Kohut claims that even normal adults have narcissistic needs and a need for mirroring of the self by selfobjects throughout life. He comments that the sense of the continuity of the self should be throughout the life of the individual. It is remarked:

Kohut refers to the experience of self through introspection by talking- about the sense of the continuity of the self- the sense of our being continuous- the sense of being the same person throughout life despite changes in our body and mind, in our personality make up, in the surroundings in which we live. (178-182)

Heinz Kohut was born on 3rd May, 1913 in Vienna, Austria-Hungary, to Felix Kohut and Else Kohut. He was the only child of the family. Kohut's parents were assimilated jewsliving in Alsergrund, or the Ninth District. . His father, Felix Kohut, a businessman, was a soldier on the Russian front during the First World War. Kohut was very close to his mother, Else Lampl, and his maternal grandfather. Kohut's early childhood was filled with sadness and solitude as the family climate was cold and distant, and his parents were often busy. He had a personal tutor for studying the classics and his teachers, especially a teacher of history and geography, often served as his role models. He dedicated his book *Analyse etGuérison* (Analysis and cure) to his tutor and to his history teacher.

Kohut entered the medical faculty of the University of Vienna in 1932. His studies took six years, during which time he spent six months in internships in Paris, first at the Hôtel-Dieu and then at the Hôpital Saint-Louis. The latter hospital specialized in the treatment of syphilis provided great experiences for Kohut. Later Kohut went to psychotherapy with Walter Marseilles and early in 1938 Kohut began a psychoanalysis with August Aichhorn, a close friend of Sigmund Freud.

Kohut left for the United States and in 1940 arrived in Chicago, where his friend Sigmund Levarie was living. He began a training analysis with Ruth Eissler and became a neurologist in 1944, became a psychiatrist in 1947, and also underwent training in analysis at the Chicago Institute for Psychoanalysis, from where he received a diploma in 1948. He married Betty Meyer, a social worker at the institute who had participated in a training seminar with Aichhorn. Betty later went into practice for herself as a therapist. Their only child, Thomas August, named in honor of August Aichhorn, with whom Kohut had maintained a correspondence over the years, became a psycho-historian and wrote a book on William II, taking inspiration from his father's theories.

Kohut's fame rose in the Chicago psychoanalytic community during the 1950s, where he was widely recognized as its most creative figure. He published a number of important articles in these years on applied psychoanalysis but his greatest contribution was an essay on empathy that was first presented in 1956 and later published in 1959. In it Kohut argued that the vital way of knowing in psychoanalysis was through empathy, the vicarious introspection. He never vacillated from the position and soempathy had become the major concept in Self Psychology.

Kohut became a member of the American Psychoanalytic Association in 1953 and in 1964-1965 he served as President of the American Psychoanalytic Association, which marked the culmination of active period of involvement in administrative leadership of psychoanalysis., He was the vice president of the International Psychoanalytical Association from 1965 to 1973. These professional activities earned him the sobriquet "Mr. Psychoanalysis". He drew attention to the benefits of selecting different kinds of candidates, including non-physicians, to avoid conformity and promote creativity. He explained that his interest in narcissism originated in the observation of his own misbehavior within various psychoanalytic societies. But from the mid-1960s until his death in 1981, Kohut devoted himself to writing and scholarship. His most important book was the 1971 monograph, *The Analysis of the Self: A Systematic Analysis of the Treatment of the Narcissistic Personality Disorders* which had a significant impact on the field by extending Freud's theory of narcissism and introducing what Kohut called the self-object transferences of mirroring and idealization. He published his second book in 1977, *The Restoration of the Self*, which shifted its focus on narcissism to a discussion of the self, its development and vicissitudes and the tension gradient of what he then called the "bipolar self". In 1978 the first two volumes of his papers, edited by Paul Ornstein, *Search for the Self*, was published. In addition to his writing, Kohut created a group of devoted followers that became a national and later an international movement in scope through which he made a conscious attempt to change the appeal of psychoanalysis.

Kohut's last decade was a time of personal torment as he was a very sick due to lymphoma in 1971 that caused a steady systemic decline. In 1979, he had by-pass surgery from which there were some complications and a lengthy recovery. In the next couple of years he also developed inner ear troubles and once had pneumonia. By 1981 he was in a state of general decline and died on October 8. Despite his illnesses, Kohut continued to work. By the time of his death his last book, *How Does Analysis Cure?*, was mostlycomplete which appeared in 1984 after being edited by a colleague, Arnold Goldberg, with the assistance of Paul Stepansky. A volume of new and republished essays appeared in 1985, edited by Charles B. Strozier (*Self Psychology and the Humanities*). In 1990 and 1991 volumes three and four of Kohut's papers, *Search for the Self* and also a selection of Kohut's correspondence, edited by Geoffrey Cocks, *The Curve of Life* (1994) were published.

The essence of Kohut's contribution to psychoanalysis is that he found a way to abandon the drive theory by placing new emphasis on empathy and the direct involvement of the self in the world which he termed as selfobjects. Kohut also transformed the idea about narcissism, objects, sexuality, about aggression and rage, about dreams, about the relationship between psychoanalysis and the humanities and about many of the ethical values, and to the core the meaning of the self in human experiences. Kohut's greatest influence is that his ideas and writings had an impact on the writings of others interested in holistic ideas of the self. He is the key figure for all the diverse expressions of the contemporary and competing orientations in Self Psychology; for intersubjective theory; for what is generally called relational psychoanalysis; and for the postmodern. Many theologians, philosophers, historians, critics and humanists have incorporated Kohut's ideas into their writings.

Though Heinz Kohut initiated the theory of Self Psychology, it gained prominence in the hands of scholars who made the theory approachable and applicable. Arnold Goldberg, Frank M Lachmann, Paul and Anna Ornstein, Marian Tolpin are the notable figures enriching the field of Self Psychology. Arnold Goldberg is the Cynthia Oudejans Harris Professor of Psychiatry at the Rush Medical School, Chicago, and a supervising and training analyst at the ChicagoInstitute for Psychoanalysis. Many of his publications centered on the evolution and development of Self Psychology. Dr Goldberg has been a major contributor to the expansion of Kohut's contributions. He is the author of *Moral Stealth: How "Correct Behavior" Insinuates Itself into Psychotherapeutic Practice* (2007), *Misunderstanding Freud* (2004), *Being of Two Minds: The Vertical Split in Psychoanalysis and Psychotherapy* (1999), *The Problem of Perversion: The View from Self Psychology* (1995), *A Fresh Look at Psycho-*

analysis: The View From Self Psychology (1992), *The Prisonhouse of Psychoanalysis* (1990); (with John Gedo) *Models of the Mind: A Psychoanalytic Theory* (1976). He is also the editor of the annual series, *Progress in Self-Psychology.*

Frank M. Lachmann, PhD, is a member of the Founding Faculty of the Institute for the Psychoanalytic Study of Subjectivity; Clinical Assistant Professor, NYU Postdoctoral Program in Psychotherapy and Psychoanalysis, and Training and Supervising Analyst, Postgraduate Center for Mental Health. He is the author or co-author of more than 80 publications. He is the author of *Transforming Aggression: Psychotherapy with the Difficult-to-Treat Patient* (2000), co-author with Joseph Lichtenberg and James Fosshage of *Self and Motivational Systems* (1992), *The Clinical Exchange* (1996), *A Spirit of Inquiry: Communication in Psychoanalysis* (2002), and *Motivational Systems: A New Look* (2010). He is the co-author of *Infant Research and Adult Treatment: Co-Constructing Interactions* (2002) with Beatrice Beebe. Healso published *Transforming Narcissism: Reflections on Empathy, Humor, and Expectations* (2008).He is the author or co-author of more than 100 publications on topics ranging from Self psychology, narcissism, music and creativity to aggression and serial killers. Dr. Lachmann has co-authored books with Dr. Beatrice Beebe, Dr. Joseph Lichtenberg and Dr. James Fosshage. He is an honorary member of the William Alanson White Society (New York) and the Vienna Circle for Self Psychology.

Paul Hermann Ornstein was an American psychoanalyst. He and his wife, Anna Ornstein, were both active in the Self Psychology movement, which challenged traditional Freudian analysis. .He published a memoir, "Looking Back: Memoir of a Psychoanalyst" in 2015, with Helen Epstein. For many years Paul has been a key personality in IAPSP and in the larger psychoanalytic community. He was a true Kohutian, in his indepth knowledge of what Kohut had taught, in his loyalty to it, and his therapeutic practice. Paul's publications, his own and those he has published jointly with Anna, are too many, but these, along with his monumental editing and introducing of the four volumes of Kohut's collected papers and letters *The Search for the Self*, make him a key contributor to Psychoanalysis in general and to Self Psychology in particular.

Dr. Tolpin was a faculty member and training and supervising analyst at the Chicago Institute for Psychoanalysis, Clinical Professor of Psychiatry at the University of Chicago Medical School, and a faculty member and supervising analyst at the Institute for the Psychoanalytic Study of Subjectivity in New York City. She was a founding member of the International Council for Psychoanalytic Self Psychology and also served on the editorial committee of *The Annual of Psychoanalysis*, on the editorial board of *Progress in Self Psychology* which became the *International Journal of Psychoanalytic Self Psychology*. She was also the co-editor of *Heinz Kohut: The Chicago Institute Lectures*. Constantly in demand, she discussed scores of papers at professional conferences, participated in and presented countless workshops in US and abroad, and authored almost 40 other original papers and chapters for psychoanalytic and other scholarly books and journals. She had focused on the theories on pathology and was helping others to recognise their patients' fragile tendrils of reanimated health. In the 1960s and 1970s when her career was just beginning and Heinz Kohut had already a well-established psychoanalytic leader and respected authority, she became a part of Kohut's inner circle. She worked closely with him, as he developed the ideas that culminated in the creation of a new psychoanalytic perspective—Self Psychology. When Kohut first developed his theory, the idea that a "nascent self" existed from the beginning of life was rejected by many in the psychoanalytic community. But Marian Tolpin was one of the psychoanalysts who helped Kohut find his way to his groundbreaking thesis,a view which was later confirmed by observation and research conducted after his death. Thus the contributions and back up of Arnold Goldberg, Frank M Lachmann, Paul and Anna Ornstein, Maria Tolphin and others have made the Self Psychology theory, concepts and practices evolutionary and developing even after the death of Heinz Kohut who initiated the theory. .

Trained in the theories of American ego psychology, Kohut established his reputation as a conservative Freudian analyst which won him in 1964 the presidency of the American Psychoanalytic Association. It was his integrity and his deep concern for the many premature terminations among his patient population, that eventually prompted him to question the theories upon which he had staked his scientific surety and built his reputation. According to Curve

For Kohut psychoanalysis was a pure psychology dealing with the experiential rather than with the biological. Moreover, Kohut argued that psychoanalysis had imbibed a peculiarly modern Western ideal of independence while self psychology had shown the ongoing importance of human relationships in the development of character. Kohut's curve, therefore, expresses nurture and enclosure within as well as across generations. (2)

When asked by a fellow scientist what had caused him to alter his thinking, he readily admitted that he "had more and more the feeling that my explanations [to patients] became forced and that my patients' complaints that I did not understand them...were justified" (888-889). Hence setting aside his classical theory, Kohut took the lead from his patients in discovering his theory of the self. In particular, it was the case of Ms. F., a woman in her mid-20's, who insisted that Kohut to be attuned to her every word. This taught Kohut about empathy as experience-near observation, the clinical stance from which he made his major discoveries. In the introduction to the final installment of The Search for the

Self, the definite collection of Heinz Kohut's papers and letters, Ornstein wrote

Kohut maintained from early on that there were areas of human experience that could not be adequately explored with the aid of drive psychology and ego psychology and considered this fact as one of the most compelling reasons for introducing Self Psychology. (9)

For instance, whenever Kohut strayed from Ms. F.'s experience by offering an intervention that reflected even a slight revision to what she had arrived at by herself, she became enraged that he was ruining what she had accomplished and wrecking her analysis. By relinquishing his clinical assumption that her anger was an expression of her resistance to the analysis, which Kohut recognized was impeding his ability to grasp the fullness of Ms. F.'s experience. Later Kohut learned to understand things exclusively from her viewpoint and this mode of observation he termed as, experience-near. Thus when Kohut captured Ms F's feeling of being misunderstood and offered a response that reflected what she was thinking and feeling, he observed that her previous sense of well-being was restored in a faster phase.

Kohut hypothesised the sequence of disruption and reparation of the empathic connectedness between analyst and patient which serves as an inevitable bond in any effective treatment and is an essential ingredient in the development of psychic structure and analytic cure. These initial observations from an experience-near empathic perspective led to Kohut's understanding of Ms. F.'s need for recognition, a need he viewed as a developmental arrest due to empathic failures of childhood and that he later theorized to be a mirror self- object transference. Thus, it is this experience-near mode of observation that Kohut viewed as empathy "as a means of knowledge also reflected a modern appreciation of the interdependence of observer and observed, while Freud maintained a nineteenth- century faith in the classical "distinction between observer and observed"(2).

After the World War II and the Holocaust, Freudian analysis focused on individual guilt and tended not to reflect the new zeitgeist, that is, the emotional interests and needs of people struggling with issues of identity, ideals, and self-expression. Though Kohut initially followed the traditional analytic viewpoint with which he had become associated and viewed the self as separate but coexistent to the ego, he later rejected Freud's structural theory of the id, ego and superego. He then developed his ideas around what he called the tripartite self.

Kohut's idea is that with average expectable care a nuclear, bipolar self begins during the second year of life which means that the core self consists of two sectors, the primary ambitions and primary ideals. As commented by Berkowitz. Kohut believed that the child has two chances to establish the firmness of this early bipolar self. The first opportunity is through an approving, confirming, mirroring relationship with a maternal selfobject; the second opportunity is through a relationship with an admired, idealized, usually paternal, selfobject. (128)

Kohut later expanded this bipolar schema of the self into a tripolar one, by adding another kind of selfobject relatedness which he called "twinship". The basic concept is that each infant is born with a fragmentary self that gains firmness, cohesiveness, and stability through interaction with caregivers who respond empathically to the child's needs. With the support and availability of empathic attunement, the infant gradually internalizes the functions of the caregivers. But in the case of inadequate attunement produces developmental arrests in one or more of the sectors of the self. It leads to structural deficits that demand compensation in ways which is acceptable to the child, but which are not appropriate for an adult.

The tripolar self is the result of the needs of an individual relationship with the significant persons within the life of that individual. The tripolar self is the sum of the three "poles" of the body

1. grandiose-exhibitionistic needs
2. the need for an omnipotent idealized figure
3. alter-ego needs

Kohut analysed that reactivation of the grandiose self in analysis occurs in three forms which relate to specific stages of development: (1) The archaic merger through the extension of the grandiose self; (2) a less archaic called as alter-ego transferenceor, twinship; and (3) a still less archaic form known as mirror transference'.

Alternately, self psychologists divide the selfobject transference into three groups: (1) those in which the damaged pole of ambitions attempts to elicit the confirming-approving response of the selfobject (mirror transference); (2) those in which the damaged pole of ideals searches for a selfobject that will accept its idealisation (idealising transference); and those in which the damaged intermediate area of talents and skills seeks alter ego transference.

Mirror transference is the remobilization of the grandiose self and its expression is: "I am perfect and I need you in order to confirm it". In other words, the child expects their parents to reflect their happiness. When it is very archaic, mirror transference results in feelings of boredom, tension, and impatience in the analyst. The concept first appeared in Heinz Kohut's work in "The Psychoanalytic Treatment of Narcissistic Personality Disorders" (1968), was further elaborated in his *Analysis of the Self* (1971). Mirror transference can take three forms, depending on the degree of regression and the nature of the point of fixation. Of the three, Fusion transference is the most archaic form and refers to a primary identity relationship in which the Other is completely part of the self which shows itself when the analyst is considered to be omnipotent and is experienced as an extension of the self. In twinship or alter ego transference, the other is experienced as being like the self. Lastly, in mirror transference the analyst is experienced as a function in service of the patient's needs. If the patient feels recognized, he feels a sense of well-being linked to the restoration of his narcissism.

An idealizing transference has the expression in which an individual seems to say "you are perfect, and I am a part of you". It is defined as the mobilization of an all-powerful object, either spontaneously or as a reaction to the loss of narcissistic equilibrium which illustrates the need for maintaining a narcissistic fusion in contradiction to the feelings of emptiness and powerlessness. The term first appeared in 1968, in Heinz Kohut's "The Psychoanalytic Treatment of Narcissistic Personality Disorders," and he developed the concept starting in 1971, within the framework of narcissistic transferences, which are defined as the reactivation of narcissistic configurations in narcissistic personalities.

Twinship or alter ego transference is a form of narcissistic transference defined by Heinz Kohut as expressing the clients need to rely on the analyst as a narcissistic function possessing characteristics like herself. Alter ego/twinship needs refer to the desire in early development to feel alikeness to other human beings. Kohut first defined the concept in *The Analysis of the Self* (1971) as one of the likely forms of mirror transference. In *How Does Analysis Cure?* (1984) he made alter ego transference a type of transference unto itself, corresponding to the existence of an autonomous narcissistic need.He pointed out that fantasies, referring to a relationship with such an alter ego or twin are frequently encountered in the analysis of narcissistic personalities and termed their transference activation 'the alter-ego transference or the twinship.'

The fundamental difference between Kohut's and traditional Freudian understanding of narcissism is that Kohut views objects of narcissistic demands as selfobjects. Whereas according to traditional theory for a narcissistic person the selfobject is an object or person undifferentiated from the individual who is treated as if they should serve the needs of the self. Kohut prescribes that the clinician's task is to cure the central disturbance which leads to narcissistic demands. He also points out that the clinician should not focus on what was repressed; rather he should focus on the narcissistic injury itself. So instead of focusing on the content of what was repressed and emerged in the therapeutic process, the therapist should focus on the emotions caused in the client through the feeling of relative helplessness in this failure. Kohut points out that in the parapraxes, there is a loss of self-esteem or pride that was experienced originally in childhood. By creating a trusting and non-judgmental environment, the clinician allows the client to make narcissistic demands for mirroring and object merging. He thus in a sense creates a safe ambiance in which the client may undergo the processes required for the healthy development and that which were missed earlier in life. When the client experiences this form of optimal frustration as an adult, his original narcissistic injury may be evoked into a narcissistic transference. Handling this situation in the right mode is vital in helping the client experience the transmuting internalization of required selfobject qualities that he missed out in his earlier days of life. The process also includes cognitive reconstructions that back up the client to shed light on his or her sensitivity towards particular kinds of feedback.

Kohut's most significant clinical finding focused on the ways that clients make use of their therapist to develop, consolidate and maintain a cohesive sense of self. This dimension of analytic experiences is conceptualized by Kohut as selfobject transference and gradually developed as a model based on the self- selfobject matrix According to Kohut the tripartite self can develop when the needs of one's self, including one's sense of worth and well-being, are met in relationships with others. In contrast to traditional psychoanalysis, which focuses on drives (instinctual motivations of sex and aggression), internal conflicts, and fantasies, Self Psychology emphasise on the vicissitudes of relationships.

Kohut expanded on his theory during the 1970s, a time in which aggressive individuality, overindulgence, greed, and restlessness left many people feel empty, fragile, and fragmented. During that period Self Psychology became popular because of its positive and empathic stance on human nature as a whole as well as the individual. Self Psychology is also considered as one of the "four psychologies" (the others being drive theory, ego psychology, and object relations); that is, one of the primary theories on which modern dynamic therapists and theorists rely. According to the biographerCharles Strozier, remarks the contribution of Kohut that hehad a significant impact on the field by extending Freud's theory of narcissism and introducing what Kohut called the 'selfobject transferences' of mirroring and idealization where Kohut believed that the selfobject relationships does not end at childhood but continues throughout a person's life. Strozier comments Kohut's ability this way: "The self...is, like all reality...not knowable in its essence...We can describe the various cohesive forms in which the self appears, can demonstrate the several constituents that make up the self ... and explain their genesis and functions. We can do all that but we will still not know the essence of the self as differentiated from its manifestations" (3).

The main aspect of Kohut's model is that it is the failure of empathic responses by the selfobject to the demands of the child or client that lead to the gradual replacement of the selfobject and their function by the self and its function. When a child does not have caregivers who fulfill the selfobject functions for him, Kohut refers to the outcomes as disorders of the self.. According to Freudian theorists narcissism is a result of the problem of drives and conflicts, whereas Kohut sees narcissism to be a result of a failure of an individual in getting his developmental needs met. To Kohut narcissism is better understood as an indication that an individual did not get one of the three needs: idealization, merging, but especially mirroring. To get a clear and wide view and knowledge of Self Psychoanalysis, it is vital to comprehend the basic concepts that formulate the theory. To serve the purpose, Kohut's insight on empathy, self, selfobject and transmuting internalization are elucidated below.

Kohut highlights empathy as the tool par excellence, which allows the creation of a relationship between patient and analyst that can provide hope of mitigating early self pathology. Empathy was not intended to be a discovery by Kohut as the Empathic moments in psychology existed long before Kohut. Actually Kohut posited that empathy in psychology should be acknowledged as a powerful therapeutic tool, extending beyond and enabling empathy to be described, taught, and used more actively. According to Ruddolf Susske:

Kohut is indefatigable in stressing the role of empathy, that is, sympathetic understanding of the introspection of the other. Though he never says exactly what it is. Kohut intends empathy not only as a therapeutic agent, but also as an instrument of theoretical knowledge; in many places in Kohut's writings it even becomes a model of social conduct. (2)

Empathy, which Kohut called "vicarious introspecttion," allows the therapist to reach conclusions sooner and there is also a stronger bond between patient and therapist, making the patient feel more fundamentally understood. According to Kohut, the implicit bond of empathy itself has a curative effect and especially when it is surrounded by an attitude of the need to cure directly.

Kohut maintained that parents' failures to empathize with their children and the responses of their children to these failures were the reason behind all psychopathology. For Kohut, the loss of selfobject leaves the individual into a pathetic, lethargic and empty life, without vitality. He also maintained that for the infant to move from grandiose to the cohesive self and beyond, meant a slow process of disillusionment with fantasies of omnipotence, mediated by the parents: This process of gradual disenchantment requires that the infant's caretakers be empathetically attuned to the infant's needs.

Kohut defines the self as a depth psychological concept that refers to the core of the personality made up of various constituents in the interplay with the child's earliest selfobject. The self has a structure within the mind and the content of the mental apparatus which has continuity in time and enduring. It is also an experience- near psychoanalytic abstraction which has a psychic location. Self, the recipient of impressions and an initiation of action, contains the basic layer of the personality from which emanate the striving for power and success, its central idealized goals:, the basic talents and skills that mediate between ambitions and ideals which are attached to the sense of being a unit in time and space.

According to Kohut the self whether conceived within the framework of the psychology of self as a specific structure in the mental apparatus or as the center of the individual's psychological universe is not knowable in its essence in reality. Only introspectively and empathically, the perceived psychological manifestations could be understood. He also states that self is not a concept of abstract science, but it is a generalization derived from empirical data: the data concerning the way in which the set of introspectively and empathically perceived inner experience which is later established as "I" is gradually established. The most important of all is that the characteristic vicissitudes of this experience of an individual can be observed and also the various cohesive forms which can demonstrate the several constituents that make up the self can be described which would help explaining their genesis and function. As a result, the therapist can distinguish between various self on the basis of the predominance of the constituent self. Kohut defines the function of self as:

A self consists of a person's nuclear ambitions and ideals in cooperation with certain groups of talents and skills. These inner attributes must be sufficiently strong and consolidated in order to be able to function as a more or less self-propelling, self- directed and self- sustaining unit which provides a central purpose to the personality and gives a sense of to a person's life. Or, in other words (genetically speaking): A self can be said to be established at that point (in an analysis) "when the selfobject (and their functions) have been sufficiently transformed into psychological structures so that they function to a certain extent...independently in conformity with self- generated patterns of initiative(ambitions) and inner guidance(ideals). (133)

Kohut states that the development of a healthy self occurs along three axes: a) the grandiosity axis; b) the idealization axis, and c) the alter-ego-connectedness axis. In self psychology, healthy psychic development results from normative development along each of these three axes. The grandiosity axis refers to the ability of the individual to sustain a stable sense of self-esteem, develop ambitions and purposes. In this axis, the individual needs the self- object to mirror him or her, a kind of feedback in which the individual is praised for their traits and accomplishments. Kohut illustrated that children need caregivers who celebrate and admire them, their achievements and accomplishments. When this role is perfectly fulfilled by the parent, it leads to a healthy sense of grandiosity and fulfillment of early narcissistic needs. The idealization axis refers to the individual's ability to form and maintain a stable system of goal-setting ideals which is facilitated through a relationship with a significant self-object with whom the individual can experience a sense of merging. Ultimately, the child should be both admired by the parents and identify with them a feeling of special relationships as they are associated with these admirable qualities. The alter-ego-connectedness axis refers to the development of a person's ability to be authentic which could be done by communicating feelings to significant others and thereby form intimacy. The child's environment should be in such a way that he feels to be a part of the group; to feel similar to and included in relationships with them. The result of these three axes is that the individual experiences himself as understood and accepted by others. In the case of normal psychic development, when the special relationships are smooth and promising, the three axes will function as the means by which qualities originally perceived to be purely external to the individual are internalized. Later selfobjects should become less necessary as the individual's cohesive self becomes the primary locus of self-regulation. Thus narcissistic development enables the self to feel healthy grandiosity, idealization and connectedness. The result is that the individual can internally regulate self-esteem and ambition rather than expecting the selfobject as external to consciousness to do this for him. This process will lead the individual to develop healthy relationships with others, of whom he does not expect the selfobject functions. It is obvious that Kohut believes that the strength of the child as he grows is less a result of the responses of selfobjects that shaped the child rearing philosophy than by those that express the state of their own nuclear Also according to Kohut the concept of the self and selfobject are explicitly different. Kohut further explains that self is a depth psychological concept and refers to the core of the personality of various constituents perceived from child's interplay with its earliest sselobject. Kohut explains:

The self is the core of our personality. It has various constituents which we acquire in the interplay with those persons in our earliest childhood environment whom we experience as selfobjects a frim self, resulting from optimal interactions between the child and his selfobject is made up of three major constituents: (1) one pole from which emanates the basic strings for power and success (2) another pole that harbors the basic idealized goals; (3) an intermediate area of basic talents and skills that are activated by the tension are that established itself between ambitions and ideals. (362)

Kohut states that identity on the other hand is the point of convergence between the developed self and the socio- cultural position of an individual.

Selfobjects are addressed throughout Kohut's theory, and include everything from the transference phenomenon in therapy. Selfobjects are external objects that function as part of the "self machinery". They are the objects which are not experienced as separate and independent from the self and are in general persons, objects or activities that complete the self which are necessary for normal functioning of an individual. Observing the patient's selfobject connections is considered to be a fundamental part of Self Psychology. For instance, a person's particular habits, choice of education and work may fill a selfobject-function for that particular person. .

- The process whereby an individual moves from conceiving objects to be purely external to internalizing certain qualities he perceives them to possess, thereby making these qualities his own, is one of the central features of Kohut's Self Psychology. Kohut in his theory conceptualizes how an individual conceives and relates to the external world in a way that responds to a central problem. Kohut thus introduced to psychoanalytic theory the idea that subjectivity itself as the locus of experience can be the focus of therapeutic understanding on its own terms.

Kohut emphasises on inner experience and relationship when he defines self which differed from most other theoreticians of his time. His perception of the selfobject arose out of his dissatisfaction with the Freudian-based understanding of transference and counter-transference. As a result, Kohut discerned in his clinical practice that he was not considered as an object external to the client. Rather, he found that he was experienced by the client as the embodiment of an impersonal psychological function. Hence Kohut designated the term selfobject to denote an inner representation of an external object which does not refer to an objective person or any object conceived to be external to consciousness, and the term only has meaning with regard to the experiencing person. Thus Kohut demonstrated that a selfobject can be any person or object that is experienced as part of the self or that are used by the self to fulfill a particular function.

The parents are usually the first selfobject to their children. According to Kohut, there are two kinds of selfobjects particularly relevant to the therapeutic process: those who respond to child's sense of vigor and perfection, and those whom the child can look up to and with whom he can merge as an image of calmness and omnipotence. Selfobjects basically through empathic responses can help the individual obtain developmental needs of mirroring and idealization. Kohut named this capacity of serving as a psychological extension the "self-object function." The person who fulfilled the function, he called a "self-object". Later, he removed the hyphen, and created the term "selfobject"to provide the idea that the function-providing object is not experienced as separate from the self. Siegel comments:

Psychological structures . . are internalizations of the soothing, tension-regulating and adaptive functions that have previously been performed by selfobjects. They develop as a result of the gradual withdrawal of the narcissism invested in the old idealized objects and they continue to perform their psychological functions even in the absence of the selfobject. (72)

As described by Kohut, the selfobject-function take place in a blindzone and the function does not become visible until the relation with the selfobject is broken. When a relationship is established with a new selfobject, the relationship connection can lock more powerfully, and the pull of the connection may affect both self and self object.

Selfobjectsthrough empathic responsiveness help the individual obtain developmental needs of mirroring and idealization which in turn core to the development and regulation of a cohesive sense of self over time and space. Empathic responses, from infancy to adolescence and then all through an individual's life are important in the development and maintenance of healthy narcissism. The first function of the selfobject is fulfilled when the parent confirms and responds to the child's inner sense of vigor and perfection" and this response is connoted by the term "mirroring." The second function is filled when the child experiences the parent with whom he can merge as an image of calmness and omnipotence. These two functions of mirroring and acting as an object with which the child can psychically merge becomes the primary condition which makes the child internalize particular qualities of selfobjects on the road to a mature, healthy inter- dependence. On the other hand when caregivers do not fulfill either or both of these functions, a disorder of the self is more likely to develop and addiction is viewed as resulting from a particular kind of breakdown in this process. Kohut comments: the selfobject which possesses a mature psychological organization able to realistically evaluate the child's needs and how to meet them will be absorbed by the child into its own psychological organization and rectify the child's homeostatic disequilibrium through behavior. (84)

Transmuting internalization and optimal frustration are two more functionally related ingredients in the healthy development of the self, Kohut denotes that the locus of the process determines how healthily an individual relate to his true self, others and reality more generally. Transmuting internalization refers to the process that occurs in the responses by the selfobject to the child's demands for mirroring, idealization-fulfillment and merging. In the course of the individual's relationships to the selfobjects, Kohut claims that these demands will respond with minor, non-traumatic failures.

Optimal frustration is defined as the amount of frustration between the two extremes of overindulgence and deprivation. Non-traumatic failures can include such things as the parent telling the child she is too busy right now to play, or a rebuff in a bad mood where child expects a positive response. It also includes being told "no" to various requests and demands made by the child with expectations. When these rebuffs do not demand any ego strength of the child that is beyond his developmental stage, then they can be considered as non-traumatic. But when Non-traumatic failures are repeated many times over the life of the child, there arose the primary vehicle of optimal frustration. Siegel comments: Experiences of "optimal frustration" are responsible for the differentiation between a wish and reality. An optimal frustration is the period of delay a child experiences before a particular wish can be satisfied. Through the delay the child comes to realize that active steps must be taken in order to satisfy the wish. According to Kohut [who taught Freudian theory from 1958 until the late 1960s at the Chicago Institute for Psychoanalysis], Freud suggested that it is only through an optimal frustration, a frustration that is neither so intense as to be traumatic nor so minimal as to be insignificant, that wishes can be differentiated from reality. (27)

Thus optimal frustration becomes the basis of the sense of boundaries in the later life of a child. When a child repeatedly experiences a parent not responding to demands for immediate gratification or soothing, the child internalises that he must find inner sources to soothe and comfort him. As a result the totality of non-traumatic failures together with mirroring and idealization-fulfillment, the parent often unintentionally assists the child to internalise particular qualities essential to mature development. When non-traumatic frustration repeatedly occurs, a healthily developing child will withdraw the attribution of magical qualities to the selfobject, usually a parent, and develop his own inner structure. This internalization of projected qualities occurs in the responses of the selfobject to the child, including the many non-traumatic failures in empathic response. These responses lead to the gradual replacement of the selfobject and their functions by a self and its functions. Thus Transmuting internalization can be viewed as the process by which the child gradually replaces the selfobject with the self. Kohut considered the successful maturation of the idealized parental imago as a process of transmuting internalization.

As a result of transmuting internalization, the individual become less dependent on external sources of self-regulation and relate to others without demanding that they fulfill selfobject functions. Transmuting internalization thus refers to the complex shift where the individual decreases his reliance on an idealized image of the selfobject in which he invests certain qualities, and increases his reliance on qualities and functions he has internalized and learned to fulfill on his own.

Kohut attempted to explain how a sense of self-cohesion, or its absence, is developed in the context of interpersonal relationships with the significant others. He also stressed the significance of these relationships for endorsing a person's sense of self-cohesion. In his view the development of the cohesive self depends on the receptiveness and responsiveness of the significant others for maintaining and reinforcing what Kohut called healthy narcissism. In the stage of infancy, the child's self is immature, and he or she relies totally on caregivers as external sources of self-cohesion. But this dependence on the significant others is condensed in later phases of the development of a child when a cohesive self is consolidated and an individual is acapable to acquire self regulation. Thus Kohut described a developmental process by which a person becomes less dependent on significant others for self-regulation. He also stated that the dependence is maintained in a limited manner over the entire life course of any individual. According to Kohut, significant others are experienced as nonautonomous components of the self and therefore named these significant others as selfobjects which play a vital role in the development of healthy narcissism.

The selfobject concept emphasizes the vitality of significant others in the process of self-regulation in the early stage of a child's life. To illustrate the specific selfobject functions of significant others, Kohut proposed three selfobject needs that correspond to the three axes of self development- mirroring,idealization, and twinship.The selfobject need for mirroring is a need to be admired for the qualities and accomplishments of an individual for the children need a caregiver who admires them, celebrates and appreciate their accomplishments.This selfobject need for mirroring includes being respected by others and feeling pride in one's qualities and accomplishments, which result in what Kohut viewed as a healthy sense of "grandiosity." The selfobject need for idealization is a need to form an idealized image of significant others and to experience a sense of merging with the idealized selfobjects. In other words children need to hold an image of one or more idealized parental figures with whom they feel admiration and can identify to the point of feeling they are associated with, or a part of, those people's highly admirable qualities. Through this selfobject need for idealization, children can proceed through development of self in a secure fashion by setting high but realistic goals. The selfobject need for twinship is a need to feel related to others and be comprised in smooth relationships with them. According to Kohut children require a parental figure with whom they feel similar and are fortified to feel part of a group that surrounds and protects them. Acquitition of this need facilitates the adoption of community codes, the development of social skills and a sense of connectedness. Thus Kohut attempted to portray the vibrant interplay between these selfobject needs and the cohesive self.

It is evident that caregivers' empathic responses to children's narcissistic needs nurture the development of an inner state of constancy, safety, and self-cohesion. But in the later stage, the consolidation of self-cohesion of an individual makes selfobjects less important as the individual's own cohesive self becomes the primary agent of self-regulation. To be brief, the satisfaction of selfobject needs make a person feel healthy grandiosity, idealization, and connectedness which gradually result in the acquisition of self-regulatory capacities. Consequently, the person can internally regulate self-esteem and ambitions instead of demanding admiration from others. Altogether the person can develop his or her own system of ideals and goals and live a purposeful life instead of expecting to identify with others. The resultant is that the person becomes less dependent on external sources to fulfill selfobject function for self-regulation. This developmental process termed as "transmuting internalization," involves the internalization of self-regulation functions that were fulfilled ealier by parents, with the individual gradually acquiring the ability to perform these functions autonomously.

According to Kohut, the process of transmuting internalization depends on the readiness and capacity of parents to act as selfobjects and to satisfy the child's selfobject needs. Once the selfobject function is performed the best by the parents, the archaic needs for admiration, omnipotent figures, and twinship experiences are restrained and transformed into healthy narcissism. The outcome of this process is the cohesive self that is capable of maintaining self-esteem, ambitions, and goals. It is obvious that when parents fail to satisfy selfobject needs, the transmuting internalization process is disturbed and pathological narcissism may appear where the sense of self-cohesion will not develop. That is, the person retains a chronic, archaic hunger for selfobject experiences, and would characterise a continuing search for satisfaction of unattained selfobject needs. Also when children undergo traumas, rejections, or losses, they may create psychological barriers against the frustrated experience of selfobject needs. As a result, individuals may develop what Kohut and Wolf labeled a "contact-shunning personality" (418) which consists of rueful avoidance of selfobject experiences and denial of their selfobject needs. The hunger for unmet selfobject needs resembles the reaction of anxiously attached hyperactivate persons react and respond to obtain more of others' love and support, which they were deprived of in their childhood.

The self according to Kohut is the spirit of a person's psychological being and consists of feelings, thoughts, and attitudes toward oneself and the world in which he lives. Kohut conceptualised the self as a mental system that systematises a person's subjective awareness and experience in relation to a set of developmental needs. Kohut called these developmental needs as selfobject needs because they are related with supporting and sustainig the self.

Kohut hypothesised a streak of healthy narcissistic development through consolidation of a cohesive self-structure which provide a sense of identity and value promoting the exactness of a person's inherent talents and acquired skills. Also according to Kohut, the narcissistic line of development is active right from the childhood of an individual which serves as the precondition for adequate personality functioning. This line of development directs a person's subjective experience from infancy, causing an infant for the gratification of needs for self-expression and self-glorification and leading to the development of an inner structure to meet the narcissistic needs and maintaining mental health of an individual.

In Self Psychology, cohesive self-structure is the significance and outcome of normal healthy development along the grandiosity, idealization, and connectedness dimensions. In other words, self-cohesion is attained when people are stable, optimistic and posses ambitions, ideals and values.The development of a cohesive self takes place along three axes: (a) the grandiosity axis, (b) the idealization axis, and (c) the alter ego–connectedness axis. The grandiosity axis refers to a person's ability to maintain a optimistic and steady sense of self-esteem, by developing strong ambitions, and commitment to meaningful tasks. In the normal development of an individual, the grandiosity axis is expressed in the sense of self-esteem, glowing ambition, assertiveness, and achievement. The idealization axis refers to the development of a person's ability to form and maintain a firm and stable system of goal-setting principles which in the normal development of the self culminates in strongly held goals, ideals, and values. The alter ego–connectedness axis refers to the development of a person's ability to express and communicate feelings to the significant others, maintain friendly relationship and become a part of larger groups and organizations. This axis in its normal development is expressed in a sense of belongingness and result in a feeling that one's qualities, goals and ideals are understood and accepted by others.

The acceptability and suitability of one's personality, talents and skills contributes to a cohesive self-structure that provides a subjective sense of stability, and permanence. Thus self-structure can uphold a sense of consistency and clarity of designs of experiences even under aggressive and threatening conditions. Additionally, it can deliver a sense of inner security and resilience. According to Kohut difficulties in the development of the self along the grandiosity, idealization, and connectedness dimensions lead to disorders of the self, which leads to an underlying lack of self-cohesion, lack of confidence and susceptible self-esteem. As a result, people with a disordered self become absorbed on their deficiencies, incapabilities and failure, and are overwhelmed with pessimistic thoughts and emotions, and feelings of alienation and isolation. In addition, such individuals may be preoccupied with fantasies of excellence and power, tend to exaggerate their accomplishments and talents, and work to avoid situations and people that challenge their defenses and threaten to shatter their pseudograndiosity. This concept of self according to the Self Psychology theory is analysed in the select novels of Kiran Desai and Arun Joshi where the theory is applied illustrating the formation of the cohesive self and the reason behind the disorder of self.

3

The Disorder Self in the Strange Case of Billy Biswas and Hullabaloo in the Guava Orchard

Man can no more survive psychologically in a psychological milieu that does not respond empathetically to him, than he can survive physically in an atmosphere that contains no oxygen.

Heinz Kohut

The chapter deals with the comparative study of Kiran Desai's *Hullabaloo in the Guava Orchard* and Arun Joshi's *The Strange Case of Billy Biswas* corresponding to the concept of the self with respect to Heinz Kohut's Self Psychology. The chapter highlights how there is a disorder in the development of a healthy and cohesive self, due to the lack and denial of selfobject needs in the early childhood of the characters. According to the theory, the early support of the caregivers or parents is very vital for the normal psychic development of an individual and also to become a socially responsible person with smooth and cordial relationship with others. Whereas, the denial of the selfobject needs such as mirroring, merging and idealization, in other words, the improper response of parents to the child without gratifying, celebrating and appreciating them lead to the disorder in the self where the individual cannot be adaptive to any changes in his life, its situation and the environment.

To highlight the concept of Self Psychology proposed by Heinz Kohut demonstrating the reason behind the disordered self, the characters of same theme is opted where the protagonist of both the novels live an isolated life without mingling with their environment, not adaptive to the changes that they face and uncompromising in their decisions regardless of the consequence they face. Both the novels share a common theme, the search for the self, the meaning and purpose of living, but the protagonists find nobody to help them out in their endeavours. The protagonists in both the novels are uninterested and dissatisfied with their environment which to them was artificial and purposeless. Hence they wish to explore and live a life to serve their self, rather than compromising with their wishes and dreams for the sake of their family or friends. As a result, the protagonists mingle with nature and become a part of it. Any disturbance to their set up or that ruptures their self would be an end to themselves as they prefer to die to serve their false self rather than to live a life in the so called civilized environment. This concept of Kohut is reinforced in the novels Kiran Desai's *Hullabaloo in the Guava Orchard* and Arun Joshi'ss *The Strange Case of Billy Biswas.*

Hullabaloo in the Guava Orchard, Desai's first novel whichwon the Betty Trask Awardswas published in 1998. The novel is Desai's dazzling and much heralded debut novel which tells a wryly hilarious and poignant story of love, life, belief, hope, tradition and family relationship by capturing the vivid culture and practices of India and the universal intricacies of human experience. Salman Rushdie says about the book as lush and intensely imagined,a welcome proof that India's encounter with the English Language continues to give birth to new children endured with lavish gifts. The novel has a very different title due to its highly allusive declarative nature of its length. In the Hindi language- 'Hulla' means 'noise' or 'chaos', and 'bol' means 'words' or 'speech'. "Hullabaloo" with its anglicised cooption into the English Language shows the extent Rushdiefic(a)tion had permeated into the writings of Desai.

The novel is the story of a young man, Sampath, living in the village, Shahkot, as a post office clerk. Uninterested in his mundane life at home and also at his work place, Sampath wished to explore. Hence he goes to a guava orchard and settles in a guava tree, where Sampath becomes a popular holy man. But Sampath always wanted to be all alone, live a life of his own residing in the orchard. When he was disturbed there by the crowd, he could not balance his nature according to the situation, instead Sampath faces his downfall, his tragic death.

Arun Joshi's *The Strange case of Billy Biswas*(1971) is about an eponymous hero Billy Biswas, a man of cosmopolitan education with a peculiar bent of mind. His questions of identity haunt him and the novel is all about his search for the self. K R S Iyengar has remarked that Arun Joshi has carried in his *The Strange Case of Billy Biswas*exploration of consciousness of hapless rootless people a stage further, and has revealed to our gaze new gas –champers of self-forged misery.

The epigraph of the novel is from Arnold's "Thyrsis": "If irked him to be here, he could not rest" makes clear the thematic line of the novel. It reflects that Billy was frustrated by the Post-Independence, pseudo western values of the Delhi Society as he was haunted by the siege of primitivism and that ablaze made him to quit the materialistic life in search of peace and solace in the forest. Like Sampath, when Billy was disturbed in his ecstatic world of primitive life, he preferred to die rather than to live a life without what he wished and aspired for. Both the novels share major comparisons basically in their theme. The novels portray how a man was destroyed by the process of individualization due to the protagonist extraordinary sensibilities. The protagonist, Billy Biswas of *The Strange Case of Billy Bisws* and Sampath Chawla of *Hullaballoo in the Guava Orchard* are different and unusual from common man as they remain as an alienated person in the civilized world. Billy Biswas was restless amidst the upper class Indian society and his restlessness was due to the loss of traditional values by the people of which he could not adjust with. Billy commented his society as

What got me was the superficialities, the sense of values. I don't think all city societies are as shallow as ours. I am, of course talking mainly of the so-called upper classes...I don't think I have ever met a more pompous, a more mixed up lot of people. Artistically, they were dry as dust. Intellectually, they could no better mechanically mouth ideas that the west abandoned a generation ago. Their ideas of romance was to go, and see an American movie or go to one of those wretched restaurant, and dance with their wives to a thirty-years old tune. Nobody remembered the old songs or the meaning of the festivals. All the sensibility was gone. (179)

On the other hand, Sampath was a failure at home and also at his work as he was least bothered about the messy world he lives in. His lazy and lethargic nature made him consider about nothing and wished to live his life with his own whims and fancies. When the rest of the family was asleep, Sampath spent hours over his books, not preparing for the examination but doing something of his own interest.

Collecting the dripping wax, soft and greasy, into a dozen balls of varying size, he had sliced through them with instruments from a geometry box; studied the wobbling globe of light cast through the belly of an empty glass; fingered the warped wood of the table. He had salvaged only odd words here and there from the pages in front of him. (39)

As a whole he had seen only odd words here and there and slips of sentences from the pages in front of him which would make him leave blanks instead of answers in his next day exam as he had forgotten the urgency of finishing the night's work and the importance of the next day examination. It is the constant involvement of others in his life that increases the sense of restriction and suffocation which makes Sampath long for freedom. He felt as if "they had conspired to build a net about him to catch and truss him up forever. Their questions ate away at him. His head ached, and so did his heart. It was a prison he had been born into". (158)It is evident that both Sampath and Biswas do not mingle with their family and their social set up. It is highly hard for them to involve themselves as they were pre occupied and inclined in their perspectives. According to Kohut's Self Psychology, it is the outcome of a healthy psychic development that individuals mingle with others and maintain a smooth social relationship as they cross the stages of mirroring, merging and idealization on the basis of the selfobject provision. When there is a drawback and lack in the selfobject need, obviously it leads to the disorder self. According to Kohut, a person's alignment to selfobject needs is an important component of personality functioning in adulthood.

As both Sampath and Billy do not mingle in their social set up, they become uninvolved, lazy and lethargic in nature as their search and interests were different from an ordinary human being. Billy hails "from the upper-crust of Indian society"(9) and "has claims of aristocracy"(12). His grandfather had been the Prime Minister of a famous princely state in Orissa and his father had been the Indian ambassador to a European country. While Billy was in America, his father was a judge in the Supreme Court. But with all these name, fame and inheritance, Billy's ultimate urge was towards something else. As a result, he is different from others and always after his own interests. Both Billy and Sampath are not the person who satisfy or do things for others. For instance, Billy's father expected him to take engineering and Billy did go to America to do the same. However, he acquired his PhD in Anthropology because that was his first love. He explained his fascination for Anthropology to Romi "All I want to do in life is visit the places they describe, meet the people who live there, find out...the aboriginalness of the world"(10). On his return to India, Billy was appointed as lecturer in Anthropology in the Delhi University where he found it very problematic to accustom to his working environment. He felt uneasy with his atmosphere and was unable to understand the people, society and its values. He regretted to see the upper class people entirely cut off from their roots simply imitating the western civilization, neglecting the traditional values of the motherland. In the case of Sampath, he was unhappy and uninterested in his work in the post office. He was blank and hopeless and so he had no promotion or rise in pay. Thus Billy and Sampath are after their own interests and they are not flexible to accept things imposed by others.

For Kohut, psychopathology is understood largely in terms of failure in the processes of the development of the self. In the case of Billy and Sampath, they are not happy with their environment and they wish to explore. It is because of the inadequate fulfillment of the various functions of self: idealization, mirroring, merging in their early childhood, and optimal frustration play an influencing role in both narcissism and addictive behaviors. According to Kohut, the primary source or the basic reason behind the disorder of the self is a faulty interaction between the child and his or her selfobjects. In other words, the disorder of the self depends on the quality of relationship between the self and the selfobjects. Self disorder according to Kohut results from a failure to achieve vigor, cohesion or harmony in the earlier stage of an individual's life. In the case of Sampath, he does not mingle with his family members. His father is least bothered about Sampath's interests, as a person belonging to the middle class, he also expected his son to live a routine life of a simple person. Also Sampath's mother could not respond to her son's love as she was bit eccentric and obsessed of food. While in the case of Billy, he was dissatisfied with the artificial upper class culture where there was not a much intimate relationship among persons. For instance, there was always a distance in the conversation between Billy and his father where they always maintain their limits. To brief, both Bilky and Sampath did not get their selfobject needs from their parents which is the basic of a normal and healthy psychic development.

In Self Psychology, cohesive self-structure is the outcome of normal healthy development along the grandiosity, idealization, and connectedness dimension which is attained when people are optimistic and posses ambitions,ideals, and values.The development of a cohesive self takes place along three axes: (a) the grandiosity axis, (b) the idealization axis, and (c) the alter ego–connectedness axis. The grandiosity axis refers to a person's ability to maintain a optimistic and steady sense of self-esteem, by developing strong ambitions, and commitment to meaningful tasks. In the case of Sampath and Billy, there is a lack in the normal development of an individual as they do not possess a sense of self-esteem, glowing ambition, assertiveness, and achievement as referred in the grndiosity axis. Also they do not possess the ability to form and maintain a firm and stable system of goal-setting principles which culminates in strongly held goals, ideals, and values as referred in the idealization axis. In the case of the alter ego–connectedness axis, both Billy and Sampath do not retain the ability to express and communicate feelings to the significant others, maintain friendly relationship and become a part of larger groups and organizations as they were higly dissatisfied and dissinterested in the environment in which they live. As a whole, the protagonists do not possess a cohesive self as referred in the development of a healthy psyche because they do not have a sense of belongingness, goals, and ideals that are understood and accepted by others.

Both Billy and Sampath urge for a different environment as they were ultimately dissatisfied in their normal place. It is obvious that the protagonists were uninterested and uncompromising in any of the affairs of the materialistic world. Hence they were unlike others as their wish, responses and behaviours were also diverse. Billy is over sensitive and his major concern was with his inner world. He was individualistic and wanted to penetrate deep into the human life. Tuula Lind Gren, the Swedish girl who understood the dilemma of Billy's life knew "What went on in the dark inscrutable, unsmiling eyes of Billy Biswas" (15). She found him "Observed with a latent guest"(176). With that of Sampath, Mr. Chawla was disappointed of his irresponsible nature and lethargic attitude of Sampath towards his life. He retorts:

"Phoo" Mr Chawla snorted 'Progress! Ever since he was born, this boy has been progressing steadily in the wrong direction. Instead of trying to work his way upwards, he started on a downward climb and he is almost as close to the bottom as he could ever be'. (26)

So it is understandable that Billy and Sampath never fit in the so called civilized but materialistic world. They aspire for something more and different and above all they are unlike others. They crave and long for something and their life seems to be a search for what they long. This concept is highlighted in Self Psychology, that if the individuals do not mirror or merge with their first selfobject, their parents; in their childhood obviously they crave and urge for a substitute selfobject and a lack of a firm selfobject and its function result in an unhealthy and abnormal self and its function As the earlier dissatisfaction would demand the individuals to create a very strong bond with their alternative selfobject. They totally get obsessed with the selfobject which could be their wish; studies or work and they would not compromise and sacrifice it for the sake of anything else.

It is obvious that the wish and interest of the protagonists were so robust that right from their childhood it was lingering in their mind and also they do not have a cordial relationship with their selfobject as their frequency of thought is deviated from them. The parents of both Sampath and Billy do not perform the function of mirroring and merging and in no way the protagonists wish to reflect their parents in any of their character or behaviour. Kohut views the disordered self in terms of narcissism as the self develops as a result of interplay between the children's given capacities and the selective responses of the selfobjects. In these responses, certain potentialities are encouraged and also discouraged. For instance when the parent is secure in themselves, then the child's proud exhibitionism will be responded. Whereas when the child experiences rebuffs, through the process of transmuting internalization, the child will over time withdraw on the qualities earlier attributed to the selfobject as a source of inner strength. In contrast, when the parent is not secure in themselves, a less than healthy atmosphere is likely to develop in which the self develops. In short according to Kohut, it is not any particulars of a faulty child rearing philosophy that constitute the root of the disordered self, but rather who the parents are and a chronic ambience created by the deep-rooted attitudes of the selfobjects.

Some parents are inadequately sensitive to the needs of the child, and will respond to the child out of their own insecurely established self. The first is an instance where a child excitedly recounts to the mother some great accomplishment, and the mother, instead of listening to it with pride, deflects the conversation from the child to herself. The second instance occurs when a little boy wants to idealize his father, expecting he will tell him about his success in life. Instead, the father responds with embarrassment, rather than sharing with the child leaves the home. Thus Narcissistic disorders result from a child being inappropriately mirrored and responded. According to Kohut, traumatic failures in providing the child with mirroring and self- object idealization later result in excessive demands to be mirrored as well as to find others to idealize which is a primary source of narcissism. In the preface to Self Psychology and Diagnostic Assessment, it is brought out that Narcissistic injuriesin and of themselves are not necessarily pathogenic, but selfobject failures in an already compromised or vulnerable self state produce either a narcissistic personality disorder or narcissistic behavior disorder" (8).

The disorder of the self in protagonists due to the earlier unfulfillment of the selfobject needs instigate them to possess strong urges and serious impulses. In the case of Billy, he had a powerful mysterious urge for primitivism. When he was fourteen, he went to Bhubaneshwar where he remarked "The first thing that hit me about Bhubaneshwar was the landscape"(123). He went to Konark where he felt that the sculptures had the solutions to the problem of his identity. He says "I know now, that the spirit was a much, much older force, older than the time when man first learned to build the temples. If anyone had a clue to it, it were only the adhivasis who carried about their knowledge in silence locked behind their dark inscrutable faces" (124). His visit to the tribal people along with his uncle's chauffer marked a turning point in his life. When he watched the tribal people drinking, singing and dancing, Billy felt a strange sensation. He experiences "First a great shock of erotic energy passed through me, although, mind you ...this is what I have always dreamt of"(125). Billy could not help transported to the other world, when he listened to folk music. The interest of Billy in anthropology made him to look at things in a different angle. For instance, when Billy was in New York, he stayed at Harlem though he could afford to live at some better place. It was his choice because he felt that it was "the most human place he could find" (5). It was Tuula Lindgren, Billy's Swedish girlfriend well versed in Western philosophy and psychology "had any clue what went on in the dark, inscrutable, unsmiling eyes of Billy Biswas" (19). In her company Billy had a glimpse of the other world as he came across the theories of Freud, Carl Jung, Adler and Karl Menninger. Tuula could foresee that Billy had something inside him of which he is not sure of. She says "Sometimes he is afraid of it and tries to suppress it" (23) which is "a great force, unkraft…a primitive force"(23). This primitive force can explode in any time. Even his drum beating had

"a mesmeric pull" for Romi and the audience as their dormant primitive impulse got aroused. As a result, a little Negro girl gets him and sat close to him that their knees nearly touched and the two stayed that way the rest of the night. His hallucination was nagged by "the old life. I wasn't were I belonged" (181).

Occasionally Billy discussed his problems with Tuula where her solution was that the hallucinations are natural to everybody and in a way had to overcome them. In the case of Billy, Tuula and Romi were aware of Billy's confusions and pull for primitivism, but also they were conscious that in such case they could only be the spectators and nothing could be done of Billy's firm decisions.

On the other hand, Sampath shares his interest of his work in the post office. Though he was lazy in his work, he had his own interest in the post office reading letters before they are delivered. He read letters of: family, feuds and love affairs, of marriages being arranged, of babies being born, of people dying, and of ghosts returning, of farewells and homecomings. He had read of natural disasters, floods and earthquakes, of small trivial matters like the lack of shampoo. (34)

As he read the letters, he picked up all sorts of information like in some countries people bath only once in a week. He would sit for hours mulling over the pictures sent from foreign countries and would imagine things because of which ultimately it would be discovered that he had finished none of his work at the end of the day. As a result, he would be sent home with warnings to complete the work the next day. Thus though he was tormented at home and also at his work place, he had enjoyed his time with his own devices which made him forget completely his work at the post office and his sleepless nights at home. Like Billy, in the case of Sampath, his family and his work environment knew that he was odd from others, unenergetic and irresponsive.

The protagonists in both the novels were dissatisfied of the materialistic, civilized world and were in search for a world untouched by civilization. Basically Billy's conflict was between the primitive and the civilized. Though he was in the civilized world, he had a strong streak of primitivism within him. As he did not want to be aware only of the world one was born, just like any other ordinary human beings, he wished to explore things and to be aware of "the other side, the valley beyond the hills, the hills beyond the valley" (14,15). The other side meant the primitive world which was untouched by the unreal civilized world. It is evident that Billy longed for reality and realized that it existed only in nature.

As a whole, Billy and Sampath are disturbed and quite dissatisfied by their routine way of living. In the case of Sampath, his life is "a never-ending flow of misery" (43). He felt that he was born unlucky because the moment he had a bit of fun, he was punished for it which made him feel bitter at heart. And so Sampath expected an open space as in all days he was able to fill only as little as he wished. To brief, Sampath was desperate with things around him and his usual way of living where he wished to be left to himself. They always wished to explore things of their own interest. Billy's interest in anthropology made him to look at things in a different angle and his perception of the other world was further intensified by an incident narrated by his father. The incident was that a twelve year old boy was sacrificed to Goddess Kali so that the young son of a clerk, who was suffering from the Leukemia, could get well. To the surprise, the son of the clerk recovered from the disease fully almost within a month of the sacrifice Billy believed that the son recovered only because of the sacrifice, as similar cases were reported from the tribal societies of Africa, Indonesia, Japan and Sweden. His argument was that if an ordinary man having received a message from a goddess in his dream, he could sneak into another world for any length of time and then return to his normal life. In other words, Billy believed that the clerk at the time of the sacrifice was operated under the laws of the tribal world. He defended

The point, however is this: is it possible for an ordinary person-a government clerk, let us say-to receive a message from a goddess and, having received one, to pass into another world, not for an hour or a day but for a week, a month, one whole year, at the end of which he may return to his normal state. If this happens, as it seems to have happened in this case, what is to be the attitude of the society of the law, if you please?(49)

According to Billy, there were worlds at the periphery of the world of which human beings know nothing and everything must be judged only according to the laws of the tribal world. He trusted that the tribal world had its own norms which could not be judged by ordinary human beings and it could not fit under the laws of civilized men. Thus it is clear that Billy is passionate of the primitive world and also being a man educated in America, working as a lecturer, belonging to the upper aristocratic class, his interests and his beliefs on the primitive world is very robust and unshakeable.

On the other case, Sampath's interest came out in his chief daughter's wedding where Sampath was allotted the duty to fill in the serbet glasses. But he felt very boring to do the work. Instead he wished to look around the house where he came into a room piled with wedding finery. On seeing the fineries his heart grew light with the fragrance of rose water, scent of musk, of moth balls, marigolds and baby powder. He held the fabrics close to his cheek and swathed lengths of pink, green and yellow around himself. He examined the jewellery box of a cousin sister and wore a nose ring. As the room was dark, Sampath lit a candle to view him in his fineries. When he mirrored, he imagined himself into a glorious bird and felt far away lifted to another plane. Within this frame, Sampath felt a sudden sharp longing for an imagined world which was deep within him. He was happy singing and finally ventured out of his room in his fineries. Encouraged by the atmosphere, he felt floating in some groundless state. Sampath waded into the fountain spraying and splashing water on the ladies. As a result there were a whole lot of confusions amidst the crowd and Sampath started disrobing his clothes mistaking the cries of the audience for admiration. Thereby he returned home jobless and the family shouted at him for his ill behavior and loss of job. But Sampath do not want his job and the desperate way of living. In both the cases their thinking had found a shape or it is roused by incidents or situations. Their in- depth anxieties and wishes come out with their imagination, interest and belief getting a definite shape. Altogether it reveals that the protagonists are different from others basically, emotionally and even sensitively. They prefer and would love to live in their imagined or exceptional world.

Being aware of his threatening fear, Billy wished to put an end to his imaginary self and confusion. As a result, he decided to get married. Billy explained:

I had grown terribly afraid of myself some part of me. I thought terrible things might happen unless I did not do some things drastic. What with being an Indian and having been brought up in a close knit family, the only thing I could think of was to get married. It was like taking out insurance on my normalcy. (182)

Hence he married Meena Chatorjee and Biily expected her to help him to get away with his hallucinations. But it did not happen because it was a marriage between two uneven minds. He felt isolated even after getting married and he could not share his feelings with anybody. Meena did not try to understand Biily and his troubles. She admitted 'Perhaps I just don't understand him as a wife should' (72). As a result Billy was isolated and alienated due to martial incompatibility. This reflected even in his physical appearance. His friend Romi asserted.

He seemed duller than most dull men that I usually met. It was virtually impossible to keep the conversation going…it was as though some part of him had gone on strike….Gone was the staggering intelligence, the spectroscopic interests, the sense of humour…the Billy Biswas I had known was finished, snuffed out like a candle left in the rain. (166)

Billy considered him to be a misfit. He failed to be happy neither with his family nor with his profession. Billy felt lonely even in the midst of a crowd. The society in which he lived was too much for him with its hypocrisy and selfishness as Romi comments that the civilized society had its corrupting effect in Billy and so he started to whine and to lie. He behaved in such a way which he had despised in other men earlier and he was pinned like 'a dead butterfly'(43). Thus Billy was alone and alienated which was reflected in his letter to Tuula Lindgren:

It seems my dear Tuula that we are swiftly losing what is known as one's grip on life. Why else the constant blurring of reality? Who am i? Who are my parents? My wife?My child? At times I look at them sitting at the dinner table and for a passing moment I cannot decide who they are or what accident of creation has brought us together. (97)

In the case of Sampath, he loved his mother Kulfi. She was the only person whom he was very close with, who was obsessed with food and it had grown more peculiar in her as the years had passed. She was considered a little eccentric as she was always in her own world. She was unable to help Sampath out of his problems because she herself is not steady of what she is doing. She knew that Sampath was depressed, but was unaware of the solution. Rumina Sethi comments on Sampath's terror of loneliness. She explains: engrosses, strangely, with its concentration on an unusual and an enigmatic character, Sampath, who speaks hardly at all and acts even less. But this could be the outstanding achievement of her novel: the evocation of stark terror whose immediate source is obviously the frightening loneliness. It is the terror of the soul which is the psychological truth and the shaping factor of the form of the novel that is deeply concerned with the issues of fate, love, conflict, all of which are brought out through an interior as well as an exterior drama. (3)

Thus Billy and Sampath are dissatisfied with their civilized world. Moreover, all their efforts to mingle with the society were fruitless. They listened to their inner self and their urge to live as they desired had become stronger. In the case of Sampath, it was his mother and in the case of Billy it was his wife who was unable to comprehend the problems of the protagonists and found no solutions to comfort them as they were passive. Thus the protagonists final effort to merge with their society and people became fruitless and their urge to get off the civilized world become strong.

During one of his anthropological expeditions along with his students, Billy went to Maikala Hills near Bhubaneshwar and there he felt that he belonged to the jungles rather than to the cities and his urge for a meaningful life made him to leave the corrupted world. He wished to participate in the real world and so to realize his true identity and was prepared to renounce the comforts of a well-established life. All of a sudden, Billy disappeared from the modern world and the area was searched for a year to trace Billy but it was impossible and it was believed that he had eaten by a man-eater. On the other hand, when Sampath was amidst miseries, struggling without knowing what to do, Kulfi gave him a guava which to him was 'cool and green and calm-looking'(46). He stared the fruit and wished to absorb all its coolness and stillness into him. With fevered gaze, Sampath gave the guava a shake and felt that it expanded and exploded in a vast boom with creamy flesh flying, seeds scattered and hit the people in the balconies. This made Sampath to get filled with a cool greenness, his heart swell with a mysterious wild sweetness. He felt an awake clear sap flowing through him, something quite unlike human blood. He could have sworn a strange force had entered him, that something new was circulating within him. He shuddered in a peculiar manner and then he began to smile. (46, 47)

Sampath was sure that he wanted freedom as he was bored of the following things as he was horrified at his father's suggestion that he should apply for a post at the butter factory. He was fed up "of public transport, of the Bureau of Statistics, of head massages, of socks and shoes, of interview strategies. Of never ever being left alone, of being unable to sleep and of his father talking and lecturing in the room below:" (47).

In order to get relieved from the chained world and also inspired by his thought to get freedom Sampath made his way out of Shahkot. On his way, he thought of persons and places which compelled him things that he was least interested about. He travelled until no buildings could be seen until the undulations of the foothills where he felt the air thin around him and the freshness of greenery. In wilderness and great urgency Sampath ran towards an old orchard where he climbed a guava tree that was larger and more magnificent than any he had ever seen before. He felt that silence had held between its branches and the moment he settled among the trees, the spirit that had carried him so far and so high had melted into nothing and he was amazed that the orchard matched the imagination all his life. Finally, both Billy and Sampath reached the place which served their self by reaching their ultimate destination that they aspired and longed for.

Substantiating with the theory of Self Psychology, the protagonists possess a weak self but with firm identity. Kohut had expressed his ideas about strong and also the weak self. According to him some individuals are characterized by strong and firm self that was acquired early in their life, but there is due to their later circumstances. It is basically the firm self established in the early childhood of an individual protects them against fragmentation. Contrary to this concept is the weak self where the people of weak self possess strong and rigid identity. Kohut comments on such individuals of weak self as:

These are individuals whose cohesion is maintained by an intensely experienced social role, an intensely experienced ethnic, or religious sense of belonging, etc. and these are people who, when their identity is taken from them (when the move from one culture to another, such as from the village to the city) will psychologically disintegrate. (457)

This is the case with that of Billy and Sampath where they possess an intensely experienced ethnic belonging. In the case of Billy, he was happy in his tribal life where he was celebrated by the tribal people as demigod and on the other hand Sampath enjoyed his life on the guava tree embraced by his environment and enchanted by the unambitious way of life he desired for. When they were disturbed from their aspired and much celebrated life or in other words when their identity is taken away from them, they psychologically crumble and disintegrate and the resultant of which is their tragic death.

The self is defined by Kohut as a unit cohesive in space and enduring in time which consists of a person's ambitions, ideals, talents and skills. Kohut comments that these inner attributes must be strong and consolidated so that it should function by itself. In the case of cohesive self, the selfobject function is transformed into psychological structure and therefore the self functions independently with their ambitions and ideals. In the case of Billy and Sampath, basically their parents do not perform the selfobject needs of mirroring, merging and idealization in their earlier childhood. It is evident that they do not have a mutual or cordial relationship with any of their family members. They are alienated and isolated. They are not the same person throughout their life as their body, mind and personality change corresponding to the environment in which they live, that is, both Billy and Sampath were unhappy in the civilized world where they were lazy, lethargic and uninterested. Whereas Billy in the forest and Sampath in the orchard enjoyed their life to the maximum: they mingled with nature and became energetic and involved in their new set up. This reveals that Billy and Sampth were not the same person in their new world as they were in their civilized world. There was a tension between their goals, dreams and ideals which constitute their self as Kohut points out that even the constituent of self (ambitions, ideals, skills and talents) may change without a loss of the self and Ihe suggests that it is not the content of the constituents of the nuclear self that defies the self but the nature of the tension gradient between them which is the unchanging specificity of the self- expressive creative tensions that point toward the future.

The self being the core of one's personality acquires its constituents because of the interplay with their selfobject in their earlier childhood. When there is no optimal interaction between the child and its selfobject, the three major constituents of firm self does not happen. Those are the basic strivings for power and success, the basic idealized goals and the basic talents and skills. It is clear that Billy and Sampath in their civilized world do not strive for power and success. Their role in their social set up and work environment is very meager and also they do not possess any idealized goals as they do not wish to exhibit any of their talents and skills. It is also obvious that they do not have a cordial relationship with their parents, in other words to both the protagonists their parents did not perform the function of a perfect selfobject.

Billy and Sampath realized that it might not be possible for them to go back to the civilized world. When Billy on the day he escaped, saw a tribal dance the primitivism had a great force on him which was actually the revelation of man's alienation from his self and from nature. He was least bothered about what the world would react for his decision and he decided to involve in the world he dreamt and urged. When Romi asked Billy, "But don't you think you had responsibilities towards her, toward your son?" his answer was "I had greater responsibilities towards my soul" (18). Billy believed that the tribal people "had a due to it (real self) it was only the adivasis who carried about their knowledge in silence, looked behind their dark inscrutable faces" (122). Billy had an urge to possess the knowledge of it and so to recover the lost vitality and wholeness of being in the world.

Maikala Hills with its unique nature and culture is completely in contrast with the superficial sophistication and falsehood of Indian upper class society that Billy was tired of. Once when Billy was in the forest, he was accepted as the king by the tribal people because as soon as he arrived Chandtola started glowing after a long time, tiger ran away at his sight and he revived a dead man. The tribal people believed that Kala Pahar, their God, had called Billy to consummate his search for identity. This sensitive search of Billy would be an impossible one in the civilized world. So he had abandoned it and was entirely adapted to the primitive life Billy realized that he belonged only to the primitive world as the dedication of the tribal to the deity and their love for Billy moved him. In the primitive world, he was related to others only through love which gave him a feeling of belongingness which was the one Billy was searching for and missed in the civilized world. In this world, he ate their kind of food, spoke their language and wore their kind of dress. His skin had darkened because of constant exposure to sun. His hair became lighter and longer. Altogether Billy was completely tribalised and he was regarded a demigod by the tribal. Billy shared the joys and sorrows of the tribes and became like 'some sort of a priest'189)). He was happy and cherished with "the earth, the forest, the rainbows, the liquor from the Mahua, an occasional feast, a lot of dancing and love making, and more than anything else no ambition, none at all" (146). Thus having brought an end to all the modernity in his life, only the primitive self remained. It was only for this Billy was yearning for throughout his life and felt that it would make his life a meaningful and purposeful one. His acceptance of primitive life had bestowed on him the changes which made him to identify himself. He asserted" Or, rather, quite suddenly and unaccountably I had ceased to resist what was the real me. All that I had been confusedly driven towards all my life had been crystalised....i had changed I knew that" (144).

In the case of Sampath, the orchard filled his whole mind and he wondered if he could get enough of it. Sampath in the orchard believed that he was in the right place at last. He thought:

This was the way of riches and this was a king's life, he thought and he ached to swallow it whole in one glorious mouthful that could become part of him for ever. Oh, if he could exchange his life for this luxury of stillness, to be able to stay with his face held towards the afternoon like a sun flower and to learn all there was to know in the orchard: each small insect crawling by; the smell of the earth thick beneath the grass; the bristling of leaves; his way easy through the foliage; his tongue around every name. (51)

Thus Sampath was happy for his whereabouts and wished to be a part of the nature around him. Anhita Shukla and Anshul Chandra comment that the novel "describes man's craving to escape from his 'real' world to his imagined world of freedom, peace, space and solace. It is also a reminder of the chaos of India- Religion, superstition, fervor and the role of bureaucrats in our society"(1).

When Billy met the tribal girl, Bilasia, his mind had calmed and he was fulfilled with her love. The meeting of Billy with Bilasia on the day of his disappearance brought a total change in him. Billy stated that it was not Bilasia he had been waiting for but for his future and the very purpose of his life. According to Billy, it was Billasia who made him realise who he was. She was considered to be the manifestation of the divine force. Romi narrated

What was Bilasia? What is the playful effervescence of mountain stream? What is sunlight filtering through a glade? What is the thunder of a volcano of the hardness of granite? ...I had the distinct, if somewhat confused, feeling that I was facing not merely a human being but also the embodiment of that primal and invulnerable force that had ruled these hills, perhaps the earth, since time began. (233,234)

Thus Billy searched for something divine in his life, but in the primitive world he was accepted a divine. Bilasia helped him to get away from his past bondage and helped him to win over his hallucinations and accept the reality. Thus Billy was liberated from all his illusions and felt glorious within himself. In such sense, Billy regained peace and felt the breath of his life. Dr Nandita Singh comments:

Sampath's feelings of claustrophobia and sense of alienation with his mileu lead to the renunciation of present existence for the life of ascetic in the tree. Here comes into play the element which Kiran describes as 'Exaggerated Reality'. The mundane background and characters are transformed into something unique, having their own identity by Desai's rich imaginative colouring and perceptive humour". (8)

In the case of Sampath, after his fly his family searched for him and when they got the information that a man climbed a tree who had not yet come down and would answer no questions, Mr. Chawla responded "If someone in this country is crazy enough to climb up a tree, you can be sure it is Sampath"(53). The family ran to the orchard to see Sampath, but seeing them he imagined declaring them

"I am happy over here" Or asking in a surprised fashion: But why have you come to visit me? He could answer their accusations with a defiant. "But for some people it is normal to sit in tree." Or, serene with new found dignity, he could say, I am adopting a simple way of life. From now on I have no relatives…everybody was his relative. (54)

But he could not say anything and when the whole family asked him to climb down the tree, his response was only silence.

In both the novels, there are characters who understand the protagonist search and anguish Tuula and Romi, Billy's companions in New York were able to foresee the awaiting danger in the life of Billy. Romi was sure not to disturb Billy of his primitive life and his search for self. On the other hand, seeing Sampath on the tree, Kulfi remembered her memory of time when she was young and her mind full of darkness and desperation. She could feel the same emotion bound on her son and so she said "Let him be"(55).P D Nimsarkar comments

Sampath's mother's experience is naïve and surprising as she only has the insight proper to understand her son's (mis)deeds secretly. In the orchard, as her son does, she finds space for her eccentricities, the space, where she could make some revelations. Sampath she knew why he was sitting in the tree. It was the right place for him to be, that is where he belonged. (78)

Thus Kulfi in the case of Sampath and Tuula and Romi ,the companions of Billy knew the protagonists better and could realize that they could never be changed other than by themselves.

In order to rescue Sampath, the family called a physician who diagnosed that nothing is wrong with him but only God could bring him down the tree. The family went to homeopathic, ayurvedic doctors and naturopath, but there was no change in Sampath. In the case of Billy, the family searched for him almost a year and at last believed that he was eaten by a man-eater. But in both the cases, the characters are not mad or eccentric to run away from the family. They are crazy and passionate after something. In the case of Sampath, he wished to live a life with nature, without any ambitions and Billy wished to live a life of primitivism. In both the cases, they do not wish to have any ambitions and they wanted to let their life go in its flow. Also both Sampath and Billy are frustrated of the civilized world. Their unusual attitude is mainly because of their passion or their uncontrollable and unavoidable interest that they possess. In such a situation, they react and are different but not eccentric. For instance, Mr. Chawla and his family met a holy man to whom Mr. Chawla said that his son was suffering from madness sitting on a tree. They converse:

'How is he suffering? Is he shouting?'

'No'

'Having fits?'

'No'

'Is he tearing his hair out?'

'No'

'Is he biting his neighbours? Biting himself? Is he sleep-walking? Does he stick out his tongue and roll his eyes? Is he rude to stranger?'

'No. He eats and sleeps and takes good care of his hair. He doesn't shout and he doesn't bite himself. He has never been rude to strangers'

'Then he does not exhibit any of the sure sign of madness'. (57)

The holy man suggested to arrange marriage to Sampath, but the family's effort to match a girl to Sampath became useless as Sampath had never felt comfortable among people and he wanted to live his life alone in the orchard shouting 'Go on, go on. Leave me to mine.'(66) Also Billy was lonely among his family and society. His marital incompatibility made Billy isolated and alienated. The protagonists consider themselves a misfit in their society and so they become lazy and lethargic.

Finally, Sampath in the orchard believed that he was in the right place. Like how Billy was considered to be a demi god by the tribal people, Sampath was believed to be a hermit. It happened that in the orchard, when Sampath saw persons to whom he had delievered letters, he remembered their secrets like that of Mr. Singh who was blackmailed by the decoits and Ratan Singh who had been using special hair oil to no effort. So when he uttered their secrets people were surprised and they were carrying the news to Shahkot. Soon people believed that Sampath was more than an ordinary mortal and they said that they had detected a rare spirit in his eyes. The story of Sampath had even reached the local news bureau which published:

'Fleeing duties at the Shahkot post office, a clerk has been reported to have settled in a large guava tree. According to popular speculation, he is one of an unusual spiritual nature, his child-like ways being coupled with unfathomable wisdom'. There it was- a modest column introducing Sampath to the world. (67)

Thus the column made Sampath and the orchard famous and no

longer the crowd mocked or sympathised him for his behaviour, nature and attitude.

Mr. Chawla wished to make use of this opportunity in full swing for the betterment of his family and so to make his fortune. So Mr Chawla stopped berating Sampath for climbing up the tree and turned his attention to make his son more comfortable on the tree. B Mahanta in his article,"Kiran Desai's Hullabaloo in the Guava Orchard; Some Exoticism" comments that the novel: effectively exposes the weird sense of propriety and logic of the middle- class Indian. The Indian sense of religiosity is Desai's main target of satire. In India anything sells in the name of religion. Religion in fact is the most lucrative business here, and involves the least number of risk factors...Desai vividly brings out the skillful modus operandi of the making of a saint in our country. There are fool-proof business tricks involved in the trade, complete with production, advertisement and selling arts, from recycled coconuts to picture postcards of the Baba to limited visiting hour.(1)

To make the fullest use of the situation, the family settled in the orchard itself. The family took efforts to provide a better environment to Sampath so that he could greet the visitors comfortably. Sampath was provided a string cot and a garden umbrella which ran big enough to shield Sampath and his cot on the tree. There was a rope livering system by which Sampath was provided hot water to bath and food to eat. Finally Sampath said "I'm comfortable" (70) as he found everything to his satisfaction.

To get the blessings of Sampath, people came in large number to the orchard and Sampath came to be known as "the sermon in the guava orchard" (73) where he responded to people queries with charm and wit. Sampath felt that he had acquired new position of power giving advice to the people and he himself was impressed by the details he had collected while working in the post office. Whereas Ammaji and Kulfi were proud of Sampath to whom the crowd listened to his every word. He was asked from home matters to the matters of God to which he answered with charm. For instance

Which is the better way to realize God? The way of devotion or the way of Knowledge?

The question came fast and furious.

'Some people can only digest fish cooked in a light curry. Others are of a sour disposition and should not eat picked fish. In the south they enjoy fish cooked with coconut water. I myself have a preference for pomfret in a sauce of chilli and tamarind thickened with gram flour'. (76)

In the orchard, the family bothered Sampath a lot, whereas Pinky, Sampaths sister, was left unnoticed. Ammaji, Sampath's grandmother, was looking after the store which sells and resells offerings made by people to Sampath. In the case of Kulfi, she was happy in the orchard where there was no need to reconcile with her wild dreams. In Shahkot, Kulfi was dissatisfied with the usual ingredients and "the kitchen was too small for the scale of operation she desired" (77). But in the orchard, she does not have any hold where she gave colours to all her imagination. She cooked outdoors under the sky and felt that "she was on the brink of something enormous" (78). In the orchard, Kulfi cooked only for Sampath working all day trying meals of such flavour and rarity that others could only merely guess and felt that only Sampath's judgment has to be traited. Also Sampath would eat what Kulfi made and nod with admiration. As a whole, Sampath was comfortable and happy. On the other hand Billy recognized his individuality which led to the realization of 'being' in him. Obviously, the recognition and realization brightened his dark soul and his quest for the self has begun. At last, Billy was liberated from the dreams and hallucinations. As a result Billy regained a new knowledge of nature and his self which made him to view the world and its creature from a different standpoint. According to Urmil, the critic, Billy represents "The predicament of the seeker-who am I? Where am I from? And he oscillates between the modern and the primitive. The basic emphasis is on spiritual awakening and reintegration with the 'self' (42).

In the situation of Sampath, he had left Shahkot for the orchard to liberate himself from his mundane uninterested life. But he was followed by his family and later by the crowd regarding him a holy man. In such a situtation always Kulfi bothered Sampath's emotions and sentiments, whereas Mr. Chawla thought to make the family's fortune using Sampath's popularity. In a month, Mr. Chawla made all living arrangement for his family to live in comfort in the orchard. He opened a new bank account where fund flowed and approached businesses that encouraged the popularity of the orchard. Mr. Chawla wished everything to be simple and pure as people respected Sampath for his austerity and simple life. He thought to divert the people's mind in religious matters and so donations would pool in. Altogether Sampath's nature words and the atmosphere in the orchard made him the Baba in the treetop hermitage. But his reputation grew until the monkeys arrived to the orchard.

When the monkeys first arrived to the orchard, they looked upon Sampath as a strange member of another species whom they spotted up in their usual domain. At the beginning, the monkeys maintained a wary distance from Sampath but he was glad that he had got yet another distraction. When Sampath turned their dirty game right back on themshouting, howling and rolling his eyes, the monkeys felt a mutual satisfaction and soon they drew closer to Sampath realizing that he was not a threat to them. The monkeys were impressed and identified Sampath "as the nucleus of this bountiful community they had come upon" (107) and he was endowed with elevated status within the hierarchy of monkey. He was given the freshest fruits and the best nuts, and Sampath too shared his cot with the cinema monkey, the head of the monkeys. As a result the monkeys no longer spent their time scavenging in the market, stealing from the shops and terrorizing the women there as they had realized that they could obtain their food easily by sitting near Sampath. He too enjoyed the monkeys' attention and became used to their tug or scratch. The attachment of the monkeys towards Sampath made the crowd amaze that the Baba had subdued the monkeys by casting his spell upon them. Though the visitors were happy about the monkey's arrival, Mr. Chawla found the monkeys to be troublesome because he cannot resell the offerings given by the visitors as the monkeys ate everything. And also Kulfi was worried about her kitchen and she began to store everything very carefully.

Meanwhile Mr. Chawla hatched a new idea to print the photographs of Sampath in hundreds and so to make Sampath and the orchard popular which proved to be a success. His photograph was even printed in the Times of India with the title 'The Baba of Shahkot in his Tree Abode' (119) and after this article letters began to come to Sampath from thousands all over the country of pleas of help and questions. Consequently the family's bank account was growing by leaps and bounds.

A month after their arrival in the orchard, the monkeys developed an unquenchable interest in liquor which brought in a lot of chaos in the orchard. Peanuts and bananas did not matter to them any more as they were crazy after alcohol and they were resurfacing their old bazaar habits "of thievery and assault in the midst of public outcry" (124) in search for alcohol. Subsequently, the travelers and pilgrims hesitated to visit the orchard for fear of being bitten by the monkeys as their behavior became very worse like:

When the pilgrims shook their fists at them, they shook their fists back and jeered loudly. As soon as they were clapped and shoed from one place, they appeared doing something worse in another. It was like warfare. They mimicked the pilgrims and lined up along with them by Sampath's tree, smacking each other with glee as they waited for his blessing. (124,125)

After all these unfortunate events Mr. Chawla thought to build a proper hermitage as the problem of the monkeys were getting out of hand. Mr. Chawla wished to commercialise the popularity of Sampath. But on the other hand Sampath expected to live a life of his own with his dreams and desires and so his only answer to his father was "I am not going to live anywhere but in this tree" (127). Sampath always wanted to be alone and for that he left Shahkot but in turn he was followed by his family to the orchard. To him his mother, monkeys and he were a band together. So he bothered the monkeys and wished that they behave belter but the conditions became even worse. The monkeys turned everything upside down in the orchard and the devotees were worried that they would be chased, robbed and even bitten by the monkeys. Realising that things had gone too far and something had to be done to put an end to the troublesome monkeys, Mr. Chawla met the top authorities in Shahkot.

The monkeys were unconcerned about the damages but bothered their success alone. Hence it becomes dangerous to walk alone through the market road and the people were expecting a working solution for this problem. There were issues for and against the monkeys and so there was a serious law and order problem in Shahkot of the religious degree. Whereas Sampath thought that all the fun, teasing and game would disappear from his life if the monkeys were removed from the orchard. To him the tree was such a good home where he had seen the world for the first time in clarity. He felt the orchard enlightened with glory. Sampath expresses: Weightless here, rocked by this lambent light, lapped by the swell of flower and grass, of leaves as rich as fruit, being warmed to their different scents. All about him the hills rose darkly up into a sky that stretched like a sea, white-stippled and warm, to the very rim of his eyes (143).

Thus Sampath wished to imprint every detail of his surroundings within himself as he was so greedy for it. He wanted the forest to swallow him in its wilderness and so he can leave his family and devotees. But he was not ready to leave the monkeys and felt pity for them though

Mr Chawla was determined to remove the monkeys from the orchard. At last Sampath realized that he was trapped and wanted to escape. In aspiration of peace, he came to the orchard, but the buzz of angry voices that he listened to in the town was creeping up upon him in the orchard. More than anything Sampath's very thought to miss the company of monkeys made him feel terrible. The author narrates and now they are getting rid of his favourite company in the orchard. Didn't they know how fond he was of the monkeys? And didn't they know how little he cared for all of them? Why didn't they take their advertising, their noise and dirt, their cars and buses and trucks, why didn't they take their little minds and leave him to his peace and quiet, to his beloved monkeys, to his beautiful landscape that was being so dirtily and shoddily defaced? (181, 182)

To Billy the real world was the tribal world with Bilasia and to Sampath it was the orchard with the monkeys. They were happy in their desired environment which glorified their self. They do not wish the civilized world to disturb them of whom they are unfortunately followed by. In the case of Billy, he had no equivalent in the civilized world and he met his tragic end due to the urge to lead a meaningful life. It was his self and individuality which meant everything to him than anything else. In the case of Sampath, he remembered his early wonderful days in the orchard and could find no solution to the issues. Therefore Sampath remained helpless, as there was nobody to listen to him.

In the case of Billy, when everybody had given up searching him, Romi, the district collector and Billy's friend did not give up. On a tour to Maikala Range, he happened to see Billy to whom Billy revealed that he had been drawn by an urge towards the tribal people and had settled to a primitive existence. Romi too observed the divine force of Billy as he cured his wife Situ from a painful migraine. His wife compelled Romi to pass on the information about Billy to Billy's father and Meena. Romi refused to deceive Bily as he knew the stubborn nature of Billy who said 'if they ever get hold of me, they will not leave me alone. And you know what have it will play with my life here' (208) and also Romi predicted that something seriously would happen if Billy was disturbed. In spite of his warning, the government machinery was put to retrieve Billy. An IAS officer, Mr Rele, was appointed to execute the plan, whose approach was mechanical devoid of any understanding of human psyche. The more Romi tried to convince them, the more they put their efforts to trace Billy. Thus the search of Billy was turned 'into a man-hunt' (232) where the tribal people joined together and faced the encounter. But Billy speared down a constable and was shot dead. Thus Billy met with his own end due to his urge to lead a meaningful life. Though he is dead, Billy has succeeded with his determined self. He felt that it is better to live a meaningful primitive life than a meaningless life in the modern world without self and individuality. To serve the purpose Billy was ready to sacrifice his life. R S Pathak remarked: Efforts to bring Billy back to civilization by capturing him by police force only lead to the final tragedy. He pays with his life for not confirming to the norms of the urban civilization- for daring to step out of its stifling confines' and, as the novelist concludes. The Strange Case of Billy Biswas had...been disposed of in the only manner that a humdrum society knows of disposing its rebels, its seers, its true lovers. (51)

The truth that Romi deeply grieved is that they had killed not a man, but' one of the numerous man-god of the primitive pantheon' (236). According to Romi, Billy had no equivalent in the civilized world. He reflected Billy's last minute:

'Billy', I cried. 'Billy'

He opened his fast-glazing eyes for a moment and appeared to look at me.

'You bastards' he said hoarsely. Then he died. (236)

Billy was capable of facing the crisis of his life with absolute self- esteem. As Billy had once told Romi before the lives of each one of us sooner or later, at one time of life or another a phantom appears. Some, awed, pray for it to withdraw, however, who can do naught but grapple with such faceless tempters and chase them to the very ends of the earth. These last…run the most terrible of perils, that man is capable of. (7, 8)

It is obvious that Billy belongs to the third category of rebels, and his deep concern for his self and soul prompted Billy to abandon himself. His death cannot be considered a failure, it is his victory to his determined self which is the same case with that of Sampath.

The crisis happened on the day to put an end to the monkeys. When Sampath was asked to descend temporarily from the tree, he refused as Sampath was sure that if he climbs down the tree, he would not get to climb up again and he foresaw that he would be put into a hermitage. On the other hand, if he stayed there, his condition would become still worse. Ultimately, Sampath realized that he was trapped to which he wanted a solution to escape. Sampath in aspiration of peace had come to the orchard, but the buzz of angry voices and cries that he had listened to in the town followed him in the orchard and he had no more peace. More than anything Sampath's very thought to miss the company of the monkeys made him feel the worse. So Sampath was ill with worry and was unable to eat and sleep, but he felt subsided from the flutter of terror on the night before the army's arrival to catch the monkeys. Sampath felt strangely calm and a strength entered into him" from exhaustion, or resignation, or faith in some new aspiration, who knows? He could not feel the trunk of his body any more, but his senses were not numbed"(203)

Sampath picked a guava which was in 'perfect Buddha shape". He hold it in his hand which was cool and uneven to his touch and sat unmoving in his hushed night. In the morning when the army arrived, Mr Chawla ran to bring Sampath down the tree, but it was found empty. They searched for him in the orchard, but only a guava was found in Sampath's cot, which was surrounded by langurs. Ammaji pleaded the monkeys "Give me that fruit. Wait! Sampath! Sampath!"(208). But the cinema monkey, the head of the monkeys, picked the fruit himself, held it close to his heart and with the monkeys following him left the orchard to a far of place. Meanwhile there was a sudden crack, a water splash where there was a broken branch upon Kulfi's pot with

"Spices and seasonings, herbs and fruit, a delicious gravy

And something else". (209)

Thus towards the end Sampath was no more. In order to serve his identity, he sacrificed his life. He always wanted to be himself and never wished to alter for anybody and for anything. Therefore both Billy and Sampath are after their self to serve their individuality. They never prefer luxurious city- centered life rather than a life of harmony with the omnipotent nature.

Thus the protagonists of both the novels encounter their death instead to face the real world where they were not adaptive to the people, situation and its environment. Both Billy and Sampath are sensitive to failures and disappointments in their life as their self- esteem really matters to them than anything else and it is obvious that there is disorder in their self which ultimately results in their downfall. It is stated that during recent years the psychoanalytic investigation of certain frequently encountered patients led to the recognition of a definable syndrome which at first appeared to be related to the psychoneuroses and neurotic character disorders which made clear that these patients are characterised by a specific vulnerability: their self-esteem is unusually high and they are extremely sensitive to failures, disappointments and slights. In the case of Billy and Sampath, there is a breakdown in the establishment of healthy transmuting internalization when a caregiver is unable or unwilling to mirror the child properly. In the case of a parent who is insecurely established in their own self cohesion may insist in what Kohut refers to as an "archaic merger", the concept which is central to Kohut's understanding of the poorly developed self. In other words, insecurely established adults may seek to get unmet parenting needs through their children as relationships are the locus of healthy development, the negative results of an "archaic merger" will show up when a parent responds to a child who acts in an overly indulgent manner to his grandiosity or put him down and fails to adequately mirror his accomplishments. Kohut comments of "the realization through action of the (life) plan laid down in [man's] nuclear self." Kohut writes "the undeniable fact that man fails more often than he succeeds leads me to give this aspect of man the negative designation *Tragic Man,* instead of 'expressive' or 'creative man" (120).

It is a weakened or defective self that lies as the primary reason behind the disorder in self. In particular, the weakness of the self was conceptualized in terms of the intense aggressions faced in the narcissistic personality disorders were considered as the responses of the vulnerable self to injuries. The self being the core of the personality has various constituents which is acquired in the interplay with those persons in their earliest childhood environment whom they experience as selfobjects which are objects one experiences as part of our self and the control over them is closer to the concept of the control which a grown-up expects to have over his own body and mind than the control he expects to have over others. There are two kinds of selfobjects: those who respond to and confirm the child's typical sense of potency, magnitude and excellence; and those to whom the child can look up and merge as an image of serenity, reliability and authority. The first type is referred as the mirroring selfobject and the second as the idealized selfobject. So these two cases have not occurred in the case of Billy and Sampath: their parents were not aware of their excellence and also they do not look up their parents for merging as an image of serenity. Thus there is no healthy interplay between the self and the selfobject in the case of Billy and Sampath. To specify, a firm self is a result of the optimal interactions between the child and his selfobjects which is made up of three major constituents: (1) one pole from which originate the basic aspiration for power and success; (2) another pole that nurtures the basic idealized goals; and (3) an intermediate area of basic talents and skills. In the case of a faulty interaction between the child and his selfobjects result in a damaged self which is either a diffusely damaged self or a self that is seriously damaged.

Based on the quality of the interactions between the self and its selfobjects in childhood, the self ascends either as a firm and healthy structure or as a more or less seriously damaged one. Thus the adult self may exist in conditions of varying degrees of coherence, from cohesion to fragmentation. It may also be in varying degrees of functional harmony, from order to chaos. It is the failure to achieve cohesion, vigour, or harmony, or a loss of these potentials after they had been tentatively recognized, may establish a state of self disorder. In such condition the damaged self begins to strive to achieve or to re-establish a state of cohesion, vigour and inner harmony. Once when the self has crystallized in the interaction of congenital and ecological factors, it aims towards the understanding of its own specific programme of action which is determined by the specific fundamental pattern of its constituent ambitions, goals, skills and talents, and also by the pressures that arise between these constituents.

The primary disturbances of the self can be divided into several subgroups, depending on the extent, nature and severity of the commotion. In the case of serious damage to the self is either permanent or extended, and if there is no cautious to cover the defect, then the experiential and behavioural manifestations are those that are referred to as the psychoses. The nuclear self remains non-cohesive (schizophrenia) either because of an intrinsic biological subjectivity, or because its completeness and continuity were not responded to effective mirroring in early life, or because of the interplay between or aggregation of biological and environmental factors. Hence there arise various degree of cohesion because of the interaction of inherent biological factors and a serious lack of joyful responses to its assertiveness which will massively deplete self-esteem and vitality. Also when deprived of a merger with an idealized selfobject result in an uncurbed tendency toward self-acceptance (mania) or self-rejection and self-blame which remain as a weak spot in its organization. In the case of Sampath and Billy, the damage to the self is permanent and there are no cautions to cover the defect. To conclude both Sampath and Billy are typical examples of protagonists who possess disorder in self due to the lack of the interplay between them and their parents in their early childhood. They have not undergone the process of normal and healthy development of human psyche along the grandiosity axis, idealization axis and alter ego axis as their disorder is a permanent and unrevived one. Altogether the protagonists were unable to fit into the world as they were unadaptive and uncompromising due to their lack of cohesive self. Their disturbances were permanent as they were not prepared to form a cohesive self and for the sake, the protagonists were willing to sacrifice their life rather to refine themselves.

4

The Cohesive Self in the Apprentice and The Inheritance of Loss

The musician of disordered sound, the poet of decomposed language, the painter and sculptor of the fragmented visual and tactile world: they all portray the break up of the self and, through the rearrangement and reassemble of the fragments, try to create new structures that possess wholeness, perfection, new meaning.

Heinz Kohut

This chapter highlights the disorder of the Self to due to the secondary disturbances with respect to the comparative study of the novels of Arun Joshi's *The Apprentice* and Kiran Desai's *The Inheritance of Loss*. It also focuses on the way to develop a cohesive self, in other words, a normal development of healthy human psyche. The secondary disturbances of the self are the reactions of a structurally undamaged self to the changes of life where the disturbances are temporary. In general, s strong self could tolerate wide swings of self-esteem in response to success or failure in the course of an individual's life and he would also positively accompany the changes in the state of the self. Therefore when self is firmly established, there is no reason for an individual neither to be afraid of the dejections that follow failures nor of the fantasies that follow successes. The reactions of the self to physical illness or to the incapacities of a structural neurosis belong to the secondary disturbances of the self that inhibit a person from pursuing his central self-enhancing goals. Also the undamaged layers of the self to the consequences of its primary disturbances such as dejection because of social isolation are considered among the secondary disturbances of the self. This concept of isolation due to the social circumstances which result in a complete loss of identity is reflected in both the novels through the protagonists.

The disorders of the self are the results of deficiencies in the normal development of the self. Basically, psychological survival of a child requires a specific psychological environment and that could be possible only in the presence of responsive and empathic selfobjects. The nuclear self of the child will crystallize in a specific process of psychological structure formation called transmuting internalization in the matrix of a particular selfobject environment. The process cannot occur without a previous stage in which the child's mirroring and idealizing needs are adequately retorted to which takes place in consequence of the minor, non traumatic failures and that these failures lead to the gradual replacement of the selfobjects and their functions by a self and its functions. The gross identifications with the selfobjects and their functions result in the autonomous self which is not a replica of the selfobject. Kohut writes, "I have repeatedly stressed ... that object-love ..., like any other intense experience, strengthens the self. Furthermore, it is well known that a strong self enables us to experience love and desire more intensely". (86).

In the case of Ratan in *The Apprentice* and Jemubhai in *The Inheritance of Loss*, they encounter secondary disturbances of the self which is primarily due to their social isolation. They had a tough social set up where they felt dejected and alienated in their early stage of life. Also their social and family background made them to live a compromising life without self and identity. They were also left with no other option as they were influenced by their superiors and their painful situations. Thus the disturbances and the disorder in the self is reflected in the protagonists where they were devoid of a healthy human psyche as they do not enjoy a proper selfobject response in their early childhood. On the other hand, though the characters suffer because of their environment and isolation, they possess goals and ambitions, but the way they attain their goals make a difference as they were not let to do what they wish, rather they were influenced by their society and people. Thus both the protagonists served their false self where they reached their materialistic success, but altogether they as a human being have ultimately lost their identity. The earlier disturbances in self and how the protagonists rediscover their true self and make themselves intimate and socially responsible individuals are reinforced in this chapter. In brief, this chapter highlights the development of a cohesive self by overcoming the disturbances in order to fashion a normal healthy psyche.

Desai's second novel *The Inheritance of Loss* is the story of an embittered judge who lives in a crumbling house and that of Biju, the immigrant who suffers in America. As the title of the novel depicts, the characters mainly inherits loss and they are a total loss themselves as they are negligible in the world. M K Naik and Shyamala A Narayan comment on the epigraph and title below:

The overarching theme of The Inheritance of Loss would appear to be indicated both in this title and the Epigraph from Jorge Luis Borges. Each character in the narrative appears to suffer some kind of loss, which is its own dubious "inheritance" The loss is of different kinds, of varying magnitudes, and intensity, and diversity of impact. But there is no escape from it, and bear it they must. (12)

In *The Inheritance of Loss*, Desai builds her novel on huge ideas about India, about its postcolonial conditions and the thread to its multicultural diversity. The characters and situations are built up with a masterly narrative structure. As Lola comments in the novel "What was a country but the idea of it? She thought of India as a concept, a hope or a desire. How often could you attack it before it crumbled?(236).

Desai is personally attached to the theme and issues of the novel reflecting her own Indian- American upbringing. She comments:

The characters of my story are entirely fictional, but these journey of her grandparents as well as my own provided insight into what it means for travel between East and West and it is this I wanted t capture. The fact that I live this particular life is accident. It was my inheritance. (19)

Desai spent her childhood days in Kalimpong where the story of The Inheritance of Loss is set. Speaking with Ashelsha Athavale in one of her interviews to The Week, Desai reveals her central idea behind writing the novel. She says:

My family had a house in Kalimpong. I was admitted in St Joseph's covent. We left it just as the political trouble was beginning, I could feel the strains, but I was about thirteen then and it was many years before I could understand the reasons behind them, as well as behind other conflicts of class and nationality. There is a parallel between the stories of Nepali immigrants in India and those of Indian immigrants in the US, all struggling with questions of what it means to be cheap labour, with the questions of rights and identity. (3)

The novel won the Britain's Man Booker Prize, a career- stirring achievement as a budding novelist; especially it is an honour that has eluded her mother, Anita Desai, who has been a finalist three times for the prize. The novel was also short listed for the Orange Broadband

Prize for fiction in 2007. *The Inheritance of Loss* which leaped the author into fame deals with the social, political and economic problem of the people in India and the social and psychological problems faced by Indian immigrants in America and England. With her deep analytical insight, Desai depicts the existing social and political issues through her characters. The novel also highlights the prevailing and common issues such as globalization, economic inequality, social discrimination and political violence. Desai's personal experience of multiculturalism and dislocation has found a definite shape in her novels through situation in which her characters find them selves rootless and lead a meaningless life of loneliness. The Hindu dated 20.01.07 carries news item under the caption "I also faced racist bullying" on page 13 where Desai says "I certainly have been walking the streets of London and elsewhere in England and people have said "Go back to where you come from" or you know, "you dammed Paki". She further says in the same reported private television network interview,

I don't know a single Indian to whom it has not happened. Anyone dark-skinned, basically from another part of the world faces this in the West...That's how racism operates and that is how they get you... it destroys your confidence and dignity immediately.(7)

The Apprentice is the story of Ratan Rathor, a Government official, who stands as an example of man exploited by the society. As a result, though he becomes successful in his life, he ultimately does not have a gratification as for all his years he had made lots of compromises and adjustments, In the novel, the flashback technique is used to reveal the past adjacent to the present. In the case of *The Apprentice*, the narrative consists of confessional monologues addressed to a young college student by Ratan Rathor who also hails from Punjab. He narrates his past to the student explaining the miserable situation of mankind "sailing about in a confused society without norms, without direction, without even, perhaps, a purpose"(74). It also reflects the pathetic situation of mankind amidst deals, discrimination, inequality, suppression and alienation.

The novel *The Inheritance of Loss* is set in Kalimpong, the North-Eastern part of India during the time of India-Nepalese insurgency in the year 1986, where the place was shackled by many strikes, communal riots and disharmony. In the novel, the Judge remembers his mysterious past which filled him with burning sensations. In reality, the Judge had no intension to remember his past, but it all happened because of his cook, Panna Lal, who felt bad that he was not looked after well by the Judge unlike other employers. So the cook was telling lies about the Judge, spreading rumours about the judge's lost glory and also of his own. Hence the glory prospered up and down the market as the cook said that the Judge was a great statesman, a wealthy land owner who gave his family property away, a freedom fighter who left a position of immense power in court, as he did not wish to pass judgment against his fellowmen. The cook also fanned the rumour that the judge, a man so inspiring had brought him to austerity and philosophy by sorrow of his wife's death, who was martyred and like a religious mother. The cook says "That is why he sits by himself all day and every day"(56). But the cook actually knows nothing of the Judge, but eventually he had grown to believe his own marvelous stories which gave him a feeling of self-respect. An example of his rumours

"He was completely different" he told Sai, too, when she first came to Kalimpong. "you cannot believe. He was born a rich man"

"where was he born?"

"into one of the top families of Gujarat, Ahmadabad. Or was it Baroda. Huge haveli like a palace"(56)

In reality, Jemubhai Popatlal Patel was born in a family of the peasant caste under a palm roof in the outskirts of Piphit in 1919. His father owned a modest business procuring false witnesses to appear in court; where he trained the poor and the desperate, and he was proud of his influence that he could corrupt the path of justice and felt no guilty about it. It was his dream to make his son a judge. Hence Jemu was sent to school which transformed him from his Patel lineage. The whole family took care of Jemu and it was seen that he always get the best. He was sent to school where in the entrance to the school building was a portrait of Queen Victoria. Each morning when Jemubhai passed the way "he found her foggy expression compelling and felt deeply impressed that a woman so plain could also have been so powerful"(58). This thought made him to respect Queen Victoria and generally the English. As a whole Jemubhai became a typical student. The author narrates: he could read a page, close the page, rat-to-tat it back, hold a dozen numbers in his head, work his mind like an unsnagging machine through a maze of calculations, roll forth the answer like a finished product shooting from a factory chute. Sometimes, when his father saw him, he forgot to recognize his son, so clearly in the X-ray flashes of his imagination did he see the fertile cauliflowering within his son's skull. (59)

Desat in the description of Jemubhai's school days presents an authentic picture of the care lavished on the only son. His mother "shook him awake in darkness so he might review his lessons"(58). The child pleads to be allowed to sleep longer, but no avail:

There was nothing but black against his eyes, though he knew it was really a cluttered scene, rows of opnionated relatives asleep outside, kakas-kakis-masas-masis-phois-phuas, bundles in various colours dangles from the thatched roof of the veranda, buffaloes tethered to the trees by rings in their noses. (12)

Though Jemu was pampered by his parents, he was not led to do things by his own, he was not left free as their dreams for the family and their community was posed on him. When Jemu was fourteen, he was matriculated at the top of the class. The dream of his father thrilled Jemu and he was also ambitious to get into ICS. Hence Jemu attended the Bishop College on scholarship and was dreaming of Cambridge. Meanwhile the Patels were dreaming of sending their son to England, but there was no enough money. So they began to search for a bride and the dowry bids poured in where Jemu married Bela with the dowry which includes: cash, gold emeralds from Venezuela, rubies from Burma, uncut kundun diamonds, a watch on a watch chain, lengths of woolen cloth for her new husband to make into suits in which to travel to England, and in a crisp envelope, a ticket for passage on the SS Strashnaver from Bombay to Liverpool. (91) Thus Jemu was sent to England to make his dream come true.

Jemubhai made his father's dream his own as his life was a simple and a routine one. Basically he does not have a desire of himself as he lived more a mundane life without any excitement. Also there is no proper interplay between the protagonist and his selfobject. There is no mirroring and merging process between Jemu and his parents, obviously the alter ego process does not take place. The cohesive self is the outcome of normal healthy development along the grandiosity, idealization, and connectedness dimension which is accomplished when people are optimistic with aspiring ambitions,ideals, and values.

Kohut postulated a streak of healthy narcissistic development through consolidation of a cohesive self-structure, providing a sense of identity and value promoting the actualization of a person's inherent talents and acquired skills. Also according to Kohut, the narcissistic line of development is active right from the childhood of an individual and is a precondition for adequate personality functioning. This line of development directs a person's subjective experience from infancy, causing an infant for the gratification of needs for self-expression and self-glorification, and leading to the development of an inner structure accountable to meet the narcissistic needs and maintaining mental health of an individual. Kohut assumes that the newborn infant cannot have any reflexive awareness of himself, that he is not capable of experiencing himself, if ever so dimly, as a unit, cohesive in space and enduring in time, which is a center of initiative and the recipient of impressions. (95)

The development of a cohesive self takes place along three axes: (a) the grandiosity axis, (b) the idealization axis, and (c) the alter ego–connectedness axis. In the case of Jemu there is no cohesive development of healthy self along the grandiosity axis which refers to a person's ability to maintain a optimistic and steady sense of self-esteem, by developing strong ambitions. Also Jemu do not possess the ability to form and maintain a firm and stable system of goal-setting principles which culminates in strongly held goals, ideals, and values as referred in the idealization axis. In the case of the alter ego–connectedness axis, Jemu do not possess the ability to express and communicate his feelings to the significant others. Consequently, Jemu was unable to maintain friendly relationship and become a part of larger groups as he wished to live a secluded life. As a whole, the protagonist do not possess a cohesive self as referred in the development of a healthy psyche because he does not have a sense of belongingness and could not maaintain a good social relationship with others though he hold goals, and ideals.

In the case of Ratan, he was a son of a freedom fighter who gave up his life for the sake of his country. His father who was a lawyer, abandoned his practice and gave away most of his wealth for freedom struggle. His father was shot dead and the situation became worse where Ratan and his mother had no means of living as Ratan, his mother and her illness were left alone. Nobody helped or remembered them, except for the Brigadier and his family who extended a helping hand towards them. The situation of Ratan made him panic. He is in no way responsible for his family background. His father's death, his mother's illness and the poverty in his early stage of life are his unexpected situation forced on him by fate and society. In other words, it means that Ratan did not live a happy and secured childhood like normal children, he grew up seeing the suffering of his mother and the dejection of the society which ultimately had a long lasting influence in him. These difficulties are mentioned as secondary disturbances in the formation of cohesive self.

The Brigadier was Ratan's only friend that he ever had right from his childhood who lived two houses down the same street and was the son of a grain merchant who was quite rich. It was the Brigadier's father who loaned money to put Ratan in a college. The friendship between Ratan and the Brigadier was very intimate and emotional. To the Brigadier, Ratan was a part of his life, a person who was very vital and who cannot be avoided under any circumstances. To Ratan, the Brigadier was the childhood friend who continued to remain a memorable person all his life. Thus both felt the significance of each other in their life.

A particular incident made Ratan to realize that the great cavity in his life was filled by the Brigadier. It was during a match in the neighbourhood town that each time Ratan led an attack; he was mocked by the whole crowd. In the end, he smashed the shins of a player and he was sent out by the referee. On their way to home on that day, the Brigadier and Ratan were surrounded by boys. They attacked Ratan and it was Brigadier who fought for Ratan "yelling, laughing, stick in hand, jump into the fray"(16). Ratan remarked "what I cannot get rid of is that moment in the dusk, against the still fields of sugarcane, when the Brigadier, yelling and swearing, had leaped across the fallen bicycles, to fight for me, me who no one had ever fought for"(16)

The incident made Ratan to know that he too had a person to depend and to trust in his life. Ratan and the Brigadier spent their childhood days together. They cycled for ten miles towards the setting Sun, swam across the river and went to village fairs to look at girls. Thus they enjoyed and celebrated their world together. This made Ratan unable to imagine a world without the Brigadier and even such an idea was beyond his imagination. Thus he felt the grip of Ratan in his life right from his childhood.

When they grew older, the Brigadier joined the army where the world can "be assaulted and taken"(17). To Ratan life was like a bundle of mirrors which tempted him. On his studies, Ratan was basically an intelligent student and he was comfortable during his college days. But it was his question about his future which haunted him and made him restless. He reflected it as "what clouded my horizon was the future my friend, the unknown ominous FUTURE"(17) which was blind and unlit tunnel to Ratan as he was uncertain about which profession to take up. The only thing that bothered him was to earn for his living as to pursue further studies he had no money. Being a single child and the sufferer of pains in his early childhood, Ratan was unable to make a very confident and firm decision about his career as he was not in the secured hands of his family and society.

Ratan's father lived a life of service and his martyrdom had left a deep imprint in Ratan's mind. Those impressions inspired Ratan to follow his father's footprints and so he was determined to join the movement. But his mother made him to understand the role and the importance of money in a person's life. She uttered "man without money was a man without worth. Many things were great in life, but the greatest of them all was money"(19). She argued that it was in that way that the world was made and she made it clear that if a person had everything but no money, then in that case he would be considered only "a little better than a beggar's shoe"(19). In her point of view it was money that made friends and succeeded where all else failed and thus money had become a law unto itself. Her words made Ratan understand the mystery of the world where money plays a major and supreme role. It is obvious that in the case of Ratan, the influence of the selfobject is very robust. His pain and sufferings have taught him worldly lessons and he was left with no other choice except to follow the words of his mother. It is remarked about early narcissism by Kohut as:

The concept of primary narcissism refers not to the social field but to the psychological state of the infant. It comprehends the assertion that the baby originally experiences the mother and her ministrations not as a you and its action but within a view of the world in which I- you differentiation has not yet been established. Thus the expected control over the mother and her ministrations is closer to the concept which a grown- up has of himself and of the control which he expects over his own body and mind than to the grown- up's experience of others and of his control over them. (429)

Thus in the case of Ratan, even his thought was influenced by his mother. It is evident that there is no proper and positive interplay between the selfobject and the child. Ratan was influenced in an inappropriate way by his mother due to the problems and sufferings that Ratan and his mother underwent in the absence of his father by their society and people who were helpless passively watching their misfortunes.

Ratan was mesmerized by his mother's words and his mind was predominated by the notion that his life in future would be predominated by laws of money rather than anything else. Ratan responded to his mother's 'oracle' as "I felt very sad and helpless. I felt as though I had lost all control over my destiny which from then on would be governed not by what I worked for or how good I was but by some intricate laws of money of which I had no knowledge"(19).

An incident to showcase the dilemmas in Ratan opting his career is that at times Ratan was electrified by the freedom struggle and as a youngster he wished to play his part for the sake of his country. When the freedom struggle was at its height, the freedom fighters were imprisoned and killed in numbers. It was then Subash Chandra Bose called for his army. Inspired by the thought to join the army, Ratan cycled to the clandestine recruiting centre in a village fifteen miles away from his village in order to enroll his name and he felt that a glorious future was waiting for him. It was like a pilgrimage to him and he had felt an elevation that he had never felt before as he was ready to sacrifice everything for the benefits of nothing. But later, each succeeding mile made him to drop his courage. The memory of his father's death instead of strengthening his decision to join the army demoralized him and he failed to enlist his name as a soldier. He was ashamed of his cowardice and wept in humiliation. The incident was an unforgettable one which left a deep imprint in Ratan's heart and mind. Ratan retorted that it is his "humiliation, my friend, and not the conquests that dominate our memories. And there are memories whose sting neither time nor words can heal. They burrow in the body of your soul, like maggots, wriggling, mocking, green forever"(21). During such critical situation, Ratan had no proper person to shape, inspire or even to rescue him from his pathetic situation. He expected that something spectacular would happen in his life which would change the entire course of his life. So Ratan came to Delhi in search of his career where even survival seemed to be an impossible one.

When Ratan had problem choosing his career, Jemubhai had problem to get into his career. He was sure to get into ICS and had a better environment comparing to Ratan. Basically Jemubhai was not a sentimental and emotional person and always prefer remaining detached from everyone. He was even unsentimental towards his parents. It was evident when he was unhappy for the packed food sent by his mother and threw it overboard as he thought that it is "undignified love, Indian love, stinking unaesthetic love"(38). Thus Jemubhai could not comprehend the love of his parents as he had no proper mirroring and merging of selfobjects. In short, he did not have proper inspiration and motivation from his parents as to them Jemu embodied their wishes and dreams, and was unaware that he will also have dreams of his own where in his case Jemu was not even conscious of his wishes.

Jemu's upbringing and his uninvolved childhood resulted in his loss of identity and individuality. In England Jemubhai was surprised to see that people there could be poor and live an unaesthetic life which is in contrast to his expected grandness in England. He studied at Fitzwillam, a tutoring place than a college, where he studied relentlessly because it was the only skill that he had carried from his country. Jemubhai studied restless, working for twelve hours at a stretch and late into the nights. Consequently he withdrew himself from other things and failed to make a positive gesture outward. The author comments:

He retreated into a solitude that grew in weight day by day. The solitude became a habit, the habit became the man, and it crushed him into a shadow. But shadows, after all, create their own unease, and despite his attempts to hide, he merely emphasized something that unsettled others. (39)

Jemubhai attempted to hide himself and as a result for the entire days nobody spoke to him at all. His throat jammed without uttering words and his heart and mind turned into aching things. Jemubhai forgot how to laugh and if he ever did, he closed his mouth with his hands because he could not bear anyone to see his gums and teeth. For fear of offense, he would not peep himself out of his clothes and washed obsessively concerned he would be accused of smelling. To the core he would be never seen without his shoes and socks. As a whole Jemu preferred "shadow to light, faded days to sunny, for he was suspicious that sunlight might reveal him, in his hideousness, all too clearly" (40).

Jemubhai was not bothered of anything including the beauty of nature of the countryside. As days went on, he barely felt human at all and finally he dissolved himself into self pity as "he had learned to take refuge in the third person and to keep everyone at bay, to keep even himself away from himself like the Queen"(111). It was evident that Jemubhai did not live his life as he did not know how precious it is. He simply led it devoid of love, peace, happiness and enjoyment. He lived such a routine or an uninteresting life that in his probation final, Jemu was unable to answer a simple question like how a steam engine works. His mind was completely blank as he was buried in studying the recommended subjects rather than to know the fascinating field. Also when most of the candidates crisp ironed their speech, Jemu had barely opened his mouth as for years he had lived a secluded life in solitude and his English still had the rhythm and form of Gujarati. Somehow in the admission to the ICS, Jemubhai found his name at the very bottom of the list. From then his life had transformed from one who had lived on 10 pounds a month, could expect an amount of 300 pounds to be paid a year. Manoj S Comment on Jemu's western notion:

The Inheritance of Loss is a magnificent work in its scope and style, in its cast of characters and in the range of issues incorporated into its narrative structure. But it is also a terrific work in its meticulous portrayal of the crumpling hopes of a people nurtured on the Western notions of rationality and the superiority of the white race, imbibed during the period of colonial rule. Further, it is a powerful critique, within its fictional framework, of the contemporary socio- political situation marked by class differences, inequality, insurgence and all accepted values. (10)

Thus it is evident that Jemu was struggling to make his career in his adulthood, it is because he did not enjoy gratification and idealization from his primary selfobject in his early childhood. He did not possess goals and ideals of himself which provide a sense of identity and value promoting a person's inherent talents and acquired skills. Also according to Kohut, the narcissistic line of development is active right from the childhood of an individual and is a precondition for adequate personality functioning.

On the other hand, Ratan in his struggle for survival heard lots and lots of promises which were only mere words. He also lived in a cheap inn, unemployed with his belief that he was intelligent, educated and cultured than his room -mates. As he was terrified by the notion that he would be left in the company of his room -mates, he increased his efforts, visited offices after offices to be "examined, interviewed, interrogated and rejected"(29). In search of a job, Rstan lost his money and also his hope. He explained his sufferings as:

I left early in the morning, without the usual lassi that I had been in the habit of having with all of them. I would leave early because I was trying to cut out the breakfast to save expenses, and also as an economy measure. I had taken to travel on foot. What mileage must I have tramped those two months! I must have walked every road of this city and, much as it has grown I can point out landmarks-buildings, offices, letter boxes-that I crossed and recrossed with my hectic pilgrimage. (26)

Ratan realised that there was no one to help a person without expecting favours in return as his experience had taught a lot about the world, its people and its hypocrisy. The disappointments and insults that Ratan had come across all the years, had taught him many lessons which made him to understand the actual realities that exists in the world. Meanwhile he became penniless and almost died of starvation where all the rejections were an unbearable moment and he had no courage to go back to his village as a man of failure. These thoughts haunted Ratan and he became seriously ill. He was looked after by his roommates whom he had generally looked down upon. Hence overnight the room -mates came to know that Ratan had neither money nor job. This incident reveals that the society has tormented Ratan in his beginning years of his career where even the survival became very hard.

An introduction by one of the room- mates fetched Ratan a temporary job in the department of war-purchases. Ratan cleverly used the hold to reach the high point of hic career. He was sincere and docile in his work and always bothered the opinion of others. As a result, he did not give importance to his conscience or to what was right. His angle or perception of the world was dominated by others' views. He left the inn soon after he got the job for lodgings that he considered more appropriate for his class as he never wished to be clubbed with his room mates forever because he believed that he was "a different cut"(31). And it was his right to rise in life "to levels higher than the others aspired for"(31). Ratan blotted out from his mind his poverty-stricken past and was least bothered in shedding his friends who saved his life.

It was the same case with that of Jemubhai, he never remembered the persons who bothered and helped him to reach his destination. Instead of being humble and helpful to others, Jemubhai took revenge on his earlier confusions and embarrassments. He was after something called "keeping up standards"(119) which are standards to his own accumulations as he thought that he was mistaken for something he was not and ultimately he was a man of dignity. As a result Jemubhai envied the English. He loathed Indians. He worked at being English with the passion of hatred and for what he would become; he would be despised by absolutely everyone, English and Indian both" (119).

When Jemubhai returned from England he was welcomed by a huge crowd to witness the historic event, the first son of the community to join ICS and so he was smothered with garlands. His wife met him in the railway station when he had completely forgotten that he had a wife, but he knew that she had drifted away All the five years of Jemu's absence, Nimi had remembered only their bicycle ride. She would have appeared lovely to him and he would have found her desirable where she was willing to appreciate anyone who think so. But when Jemubhai returned from England, he was quite unusual and behaved a stranger to his relatives and neighbours who boasted for his success because he had become a foreigner in his own land as he had developed the idea of privacy. Hence Jemubhai did not like his wife as to him "an Indian girl could never be as beautiful as an English one"(168) and therefore considered his wife as an illiterate village girl. The cruelty to her became irresistible and he taught her the same lesson of loneliness and shame, that he had learnt himself. In public, he never spoke to or looked in her direction. When Jemubhai and Nimi arrived in Bonda, Jemu hired Nimi a companion, Miss Enid Pott, to teach her English, manners and the basic etiquette. But Nimi learnt no English and Jemu thought that it was all because of her stubbornness. He shouted:

"What is this?" he asked holding up the bread roll.

Silence.

"If you can't say the word, you can't eat it"

More silence.

He removed it from her plate. (171)

As he believed that his wife was an illiterate and uncultured, he refused to take her anywhere. And so Nimi did not accompany her husband on his tour, unlike others. Hence Nimi was left alone in Bonda three weeks out of four where she paced the house and the garden. Before marriage, Nimi had spent nineteen years within the confines of her father, but even after marriage, she was unable to contemplate the idea of walking through the gate. It was all because of her loneliness and her uncared situation. Her freedom was useless as her husband disregarded her and she was completely devoid of her husband's love. Altogether she had fallen out of life with no interest and purpose in it. As a result, Nimi spoke to nobody for weeks where the servants gave her the leftovers to eat, stole the supplies of the house and allowed the house to grow filthy until Jemubhsi arrived. Nimi was helpless and irresponsive because she herself was in a pathetic situation where even her expressions annoyed Jemu as she was "without enterprise, unable to entertain herself, made of nothing, yet with a disruptive presence"(172). P V Laxmi Prasad comments Jemubhai that he suffered from a sense of inferiority and defeat which resulted in a sadistic violence in personal life and turned him into a hated civilian in his own community. In his eagerness to maintain equal status with the British, he disowned his own family tradition and culture and inherited the loss of self esteem, pride and vitality that left him emotionally paralytic and spiritually dead. (22)

Unable to give up his contempt for Indian heritage and also to keep up his so called English standards, Jemubhai treated Nimi cruelly both physically and mentally. He raped his young wife with anger and disgust and repeated the disgraceful deed. He was particular never to develop any emotional bond between him and his wife and so he often embarrasses her. For instance, once when Jemubhai found her footprints on the toilet seat, in outrage he took her head and pushed it into the toilet bowl. The harassments made Nimi sink in misery which made her grew very dull. As a result, she began to fall asleep in sunshine and get up in the middle of the night. She could not focus on the world, never went to the mirror, because she could not see herself in it as she could not spend a moment in dressing and combing as those were the activities only for the loved and happy. Eventually, the dread Jemubhai and Nimi had for each other been so severe with limitless bitterness. He beat her severely and sent Nimi to her parental home after knowing that she is responsible for blocking his promotion by being part of the committee that had welcomed Pandit Jawaharlal Nehru at the local railway station. This shows that Jemubhai did not live a normal life, he suffered in his earlier stage of life and he reflected this suffocation and dejection to others and the victim is none other than his wife.

Jemubhai returned Nimi to Gujarat where she was abandoned in her parental home and even just to make living became difficult to her. Even the birth of his child did not change him. Instead he sent money with a letter "it was not possible. My work is such. No schools. Constant travel..." (306). But the family abandoned her for it is the responsibility of her husband to take care of Nimi and her child. Nimi had no other go and she lived the rest of her life with a sister. When Jemubhai's father pleaded him to accept Nimi, he turned deaf ears to him saying that Nimi was unsuitable to be his wife. His father annoyed that Jemu had become completely a stranger and he had forgotten his responsibilities towards his family and also towards his countrymen. His community believed that Jemubhai would bring them welfare and standard but it became a nightmare. Thus his father's dream was shattered as his son himself cannot do justice to his own family life. Later Nimi was dead catching fire over a stove. Jemubhai was not even committed to his daughter who eloped and later died with her husband in Russia. The only companion that he had in his old days is his granddaughter, Sai, but he was different even to her. She comments her grandfather as more lizard than human. She also comments that Jemu had fixed gaze, lack of movements and also a person travelled forward but far back.

It is the same case with that of Ratan, like Jemu, he reached heights in his career but being inhumane. When he started his career, effortless docility came to him naturally he liked "to please as a fish likes to swim"(34). He practiced the perfect yes-mannership which soon transformed him to a valuable employee. Rattan pleased his superiors and never did anything that displeased them. As a result, his reputation grew with his talent, skills and hard work. Ratan remained restless until he completed the work that was assigned to him and never wished to be rebuked by anybody as all his efforts were for his career. He committed "One had to live. And to live one had to make a living. And, how was a living to be made except through career"(39). His ability in handling matters improved with the Superintendent's coaching of which he became an efficient worker like one of his notes drove a contractor bankrupt which was his first thrust of power. When the contractor's son tried to buy Ratan's support with a bribe of ten thousand rupees, he was shocked and surprised that the people who once bullied him were now greasing his palms to get things done and Ratan could feel the difference that he who was striving hard for his survival and career, had later got powers to freeze others.

To Ratan, career was the primary one rather than anything else and so he took challenging additional work. For instance, when a particular was assigned to three clerks including Ratan and the other two clerks were unwilling to do the work, Ratan broke away from themand did the work individually. He was also pretending to please people of whom he did not care as according to him it did not matter whether a person took a right side or a wrong side and there were no morals involved in it because according to him what mattered was only person's skills. Basically, Ratan in his earlier days was tormented between the ideals of his father and mother. But once when the situation made him to realize the importance of money and career as of his mother's ideals, he began to move in the path. He was sure of his target but was unsure of reaching itin the right way. The Superintendent who trained Ratan sowed the hard truth of civilized world that there was no point in looking for truth in the world as God was concerned only with what a person did with money and not on how he got it. The Superintendent's concept of God was strange which muddled Ratan and it was:

Having acknowledged God's existence we carry on, certain that He need not bothered with the details. God sees all, we say. But having seen, goes his way, twirling His walking stick. He sees all but does not necessarily at the same time judge. His judgement, we like to believe, come only in spurts, if it comes at all, and can be influenced with a lump sum. All you need is a wherewithal and a broker. (44)

It is evident that Ratan as a person had no individuality as he was dominated by his mother's ideals and later by the Superintendent.

As the war came to a close, it was announced that Ratan would be retrenched along with many others. This news brought him back to darkness which made him fear of his future once again. Meanwhile the Superintendent made a deal with Ratan as he was offered with officer ship as a reward for marrying his niece. Rattan was unhappy that even his marriage was a deal. He commented;

Deals, deals, deals, my friend, that is what the world runs on, what is all about. If men forgot how to make deals, the world would come to a stop. It would lose its propelling power. Men would not know what to do with themselves. they would lose interest. It is not the atom or the sun or God or sex that lies at the heart of the universe. It is DEALS, DEALS. (48)

Thus the deal marked a turning point in Ratan's life as he was secured of his job and also he soon became an officer. He accepted bribe which he had never needed because he lived a comfortable life with most of his necessities fulfilled. He reflected;

In this poor land I can be called comfortable, even well-off. I have a car, a flat, a concrete roof, running water. My daughter has all the money she needs: for college, clothes and the cinema. We eat as much as a human being can possibly eat. Our health is looked after by the Government. (58, 59)

Ratan realised that his acceptance of bribe was because of 'They' (60) who are none other than the authorities. O P Patnagar remarks that "In Ratan, Arun Joshi, has presented a brilliant Pascalian image of self-deception and self-love in which he holds himself innocent and runs to accuse others for his misdeeds" (39).

It was obvious that to authorities the common men were mere "new slavery"(61). People in general knew what was right and wrong but it was not practiced as it was considered that only man with either money or power would be taken into account, whereas all others were considered to be worthless. Ratan comments that in such circumstances it would be difficult for persons to be his own masters but it was very easy to be his own slaves and of others. This was the exact case of Ratan as he was aware that he was under a system of which it was difficult for him to throw off and pursue his career. Thus Ratan was chained everywhere by his superiors and his feeling of being used-up made him restless and frustrated. He was ultimately aware of the fact that anything and everything in the world was possible only if it was backed up by power. This notion disturbed him and made him dull and lazy. Even in such critical circumstances he did not give up his pursuit for his career. But he realized that it can be achieved not only through docility but through flattery. His first step would be to discover his superiors likes and dislikes and fall completely in line with them. He excelled in this regard and confessed his degrading behavior. Ratan confessed:

I had become a scoundrel. No doubt about that. But believe me, we were all like this. I was not the only one…A free-for-all .a great darkness.Blinding us.Andblind following the blind. And everybody lying. That was the way it was then. And that is the way it is now. Worse perhaps. On top of everything there is this humiliation to contend with. In our hearts, if not in our faces. (66, 67)

In the case of superiors, who are good and decent, Ratan would behave in the other way. He was responsible for the humiliation of a superior who was serious and competent as he came to know that if that superior left the place then he might get that position. As the haunting word, career, inspired him, he did malpractice against the superior and the result of which was a successful one to him. This was an instance of Ratan's loss of humanity and conscience. Though he knew what was right and wrong, for the sake of his career Ratan did things which would benefit him, despite spoiling others honour and dignity.

Later Ratan underwent a situation which shackled his wrong ideals, particularly his attitude on money and career. Before the war Ratan was bribed by Himmat Singh, who had a big pile of military materials which Ratan had rejected once because they were no good. With the back-up of the minister and the secretary, Himmat Singh demanded Ratan to pass the pile by offering Ratan a cut. As there were no other options, Ratan accepted the bribe and passed those materials provided it would reach the army store with all the documents and tracks of men connected with the transaction destroyed. Everything was planned and went on well, but something unexpected happened that there was a war.

Ratan's lack of individuality and he being influenced by others made him feel that he was a 'nobody' in the world. Consequently, Ratan remained as a frustrated man in the world full of chaos where there were no norms as he was completely under the control of his authorities who decided everything in his life. For instance, one of his authorities even decided his marriage. Rattan regretted that "They wanted this. They wanted that. Did they ever stop to think what I wanted? What right had they to claim my loyalities, take me granted? What right?"(71). Thus his restlessness made him a frustrated man in his family and a lethargic employee in his office. The end is that Ratan realized that in the process of adjustment something fine in his soul was destroyed.

In terrible loneliness, Ratan felt horrible with his anger and failure which made him to see his own "soul turn to ashes" (71). In Ratan's case because of his lack of the self, his character worsened from bad to worse. A Rajendra Prasad comments "By the time Ratan wakes up to the fact of his higher self, something fine in his own soul is destroyed, and he finds himself cornered into a veritable moral aridity with no company other than of his own fact(10).

His degrading character made him to feel that nothing is wrong. He ogled at women openly and felt that he had a right to do so. As to Ratan committing an evil for the first time was a terrible one, but later it had become a habit to him and he was even ready to justify all his dealings. The more money he accumulated, the more dissatisfied Ratan was in his life and frequently the thought of death crossed him. As a whole, he realized that money dictated not only the world but also the possessors. He reflected that "in money's kingdom, my friend, only money is king. All others are slaves. And none is greater slave than its proud possessor"(75).

Ratan's concept of money and his justification of his character had a complete twist when the Brigadier came back from the war due to his unusual behavior of his nervous breakdown. As Ratan throughout his life was closely associated with Brigadier, he wished to trace the root cause of his behaviour. Everyday Ratan visited the hospital though he was not allowed to see the Brigadier. It was in the hospital Ratan happened to see the terrifying effect of the war. He stated that the war had come to an end to the nation but not to the persons who had lost their dears in the war. He became aware of the vast crowd of men, women and children whose lives were conditioned not only by their limitations but also by the whims and fancies of the men who visited them, Ratan narrated:

The doctors, the nurses, piles of scarlet bandages, clotted and amputated limbs, eyes, bewildered or dazed, frightened faces, the long neon-lit corridors, trolleys carting the dead, limbs angular and still under white shrouds, caravans of slow-moving ambulances proceeding through the twilight, the bronze guns, wards filled with shadows and suffering, stark walls, the poster of the Dal. In varying intensity all these and much else passed before my eyes in one endless procession, over and over. (94)

The impact of war on the people had a purifying effect on Ratan. To his dismay, Ratan realised that his role in clearing the defective weapons had caused the mental illness of the Brigadier as he was accused of desertion and was expected to be court-martialed any day. The reason behind the desertion of the Brigadier in the war field was because at the last minute his equipment had failed which was originally cleared by Ratan for Himmat Singh. The fact made Ratan dumb struck and his vision of the Brigadier standing sleepless and exhausted troubled him as it was for the second time in his life that he had felt the pain of another as his own. The first was the moment when his father was shot dead.

When Ratan was asked to report at the police station for an enquiry regarding the clearance of defective war materials that caused the army several hundred lives, he pretended to be innocent as he was sure that there were no evidences or traces of how those materials were supplied and the officials were trying to trap him. So Ratan proved to be unnerved by the interrogation of the army officials. Ratan was imprisoned and he had the dilemma whether to confess or not. Even then Ratan blamed that he was not the only person who did a heinous act which consumed the lives of a lot. He accused the society in which he lived. Ratan said;

Why should I confess? What right had they to persecute me like that? It was not as though I was the only one in the history of India who had even taken a bribe. What were they able to do with the thousands who thieved, raped and murdered and got away? Besides, how could one be so sure that those materials were defective? (107)

When Ratan was in the prison, he was unable to seek help from his relatives or neighbours. In the city where he had spent his twenty years of life, Ratan could not find a person to whom he can confide the truth. This reveals the lagging social relationship that he maintains with others. Ultimately, he did not have a proper inspirer to mould him in the right way. His personal situation and the passive role of the society solving his problems are the root cause of Ratan's inability and nature. Hence he had nobody to help him out but Himmat Singh, just by a phone call to him Ratan succeeded in getting orders for his release. Ratan knew that his confession could save the life and honour of his close friend. So he prepared a letter of confession with enough loopholes for him to wriggle his way out. It was Ratan's last chance to refine himself, but he was cowardice to send the letter. After two weeks, Ratan came to know that the Brigadier had shot himself dead. When Ratan went to the console, the Brigadier's wife handed him the charm that Ratan gave to the Brigadier on the eve of his departure to the battlefield. She also told that it was the Brigadier's wish to return back the charm to Ratan. Shaken by the tragedy, Ratan resolved to take revenge on Himmat Singh. But when Ratan came to know that Himmat Singh was merely a weapon in the hands of the minister and the secretary, the real instigators of the arm deal. The truth shattered Ratan and he realised that for two decades he had lived only in "dismay, confused, exploited, deceiving and now deceived"(133). Rattan realised that he was deceived beyond his imagination and all his days he had lived a meaningless life which was useless to nobody. The tragedy made him understand that there was no point in blaming others because he had his own mistakes. Ultimately, Ratan was deceived and exploited by others as he had no self or individuality. He was influenced by others easily and was exploited the most. This realisation had made Ratan to live the rest of his life to be of some use to others. So he tried to do penance for his misdeeds by going to the temple every morning and wiping the shoes left by the devotees who had gone to pray. His hands smelling of leather, Ratan said;

Be good, I tell myself. Be good. Be decent. Be of use. Then I beg forgiveness. Of a large host: my father, my mother, the Brigadier, the unknown dead of the war, of those whom I harmed with deliberation and with cunning, of all those who have been the victims of my cleverness, those whom I could have helped and did not. (143)

In the view of the world Ratan was a gentleman. But Ratan knows what he was and he had repented for what he had done. This is the point in which Ratan realised his self, he had become pure in his thought, action and deed. On the other hand, Jemubhai too faced the typical circumstances which made him to identify himself. Unlike Ratan, Jemubhai was not intimate with anybody, even with his own grand-daughter. He was highly independent and after his own ideals, but less influenced by others unlike Ratan. But both Ratan and Jemubhai believed and trusted that what they do is right as they always justify their character and their behaviour. What mattered to them is their own point of view and was least bothered about what others would think of their deeds. In the case of both Ratan and Jemubhai, they suffered a period of time for their career; Ratan in search of a job and Jemubhai to join the ICS. Those were their crucial period where they struggled and later made others suffer for the pain that they trembled with. Once when they attained power, they wished to over- power others. But both are hard workers who work relentlessly. It was career which was very important to them than anything else in the world. They followed ideals of their own interest and flexibility until they crossed a painful and panic situation intheir life. In the case of Ratan, it was his friend's tragedy and for it was the loss of his dog, Mutt which had an impact and response in them and made them reacted.

When the situation in Kalimpong was worsening of road blocks, robbery, and strikes with no kerosene, gas, water or electricity, Mutt was stolen to be sold which was Jemubhai's only companion all his life. Terror trapped in each people of the city and horror grew through out Kalimpong where roads were blocked and there were curfew every night.

Kalimpong was transformed into a ghost town, the wind tumbling around the melancholy streets, garbage flying by unhindered. Whatever point the GNLF might have had, it was severely out of hand, even one man's anger, in those days seemed enough to set hillside alight.(281)

In such a terrible situation, the people who lived a luxurious and peaceful life where shackled. Everything went upside down as people had to strive for their food and shelter. In such a situation, the wife of the drunken man, who was wrongly victimised for the theft of Jemibhai's gun and the father came again for begging mercy of the judge, but he was adamant of not giving them anything. The two figures hide themselves in the forest and when the night fell, they went back to the judge's house to snatch Mutt in order to sell the fat dog to get some money to survive. Jemubhai shouted and searched for Mutt everywhere but he could not find him anywhere and later reported in the police station.

Jemubhai became frantic without Mutt and searched for it every-where shouting all the language between Mutt and himself. Ultimately, Jemubhai realised that his position of power had gone frittered away in years of misanthropy and cynicism. He realises that he has no influence in his present and his ill approach of his past was totally a misdeed which led him to nowhere. He regrets remembering"all of a sudden why he had gone to England and joined the ICS, it was cleverer than ever why- but now the position of power was gone, frittered away in years of misanthropy and cynicisms" (292).

He remembered his past and could not conceive punishment for his misdeeds. He thought that the fate is paying him back for the sins he had committed that no court in the world could take on. He remembered how he had abandoned his family, his father's love and hope, how he had ill-treated his wife and collapsed his relatives thought that Jemubhai would help them.

Jemubhai recollected and re thought if it was he who killed his wife for the sake of his false ideals, stealing her dignity and by transforming her into the embodiment of humiliation. Only years after his wife's death, Jemubhai could at least understand the pains of Nimi that her family would not have accepted her and her life would be useless then. He had also abandoned his daughter and made her life absurd by condemning the girl into a convent boarding school and got relieved when she had eloped with a man who had grown up in an orphanage. Thus all his life Jemubhai abandoned others and lived a purposeless and meaningless life of which he was unaware of. He lost the essence of his life by being inhumane and ungentle. All his life, Jemubhai hated his wife, but the tragedy he underwent made him remember a moment when he liked her. It was when Jemubhai was in his twenty and Nimi in her fourteen when they were on a bicycle travelling gloriously down a slope. Jemubhai learned that a human being can be transformed to anything and "It was possible to forget and something essential to do so"(308). He realised that his past was blurry and when he had come out of it, the world had completely changed. Stuart Hall explains: globalization continues the trajectory in making the world 'a market for the West' affiliation with the West makes a person much more valuable than someone with no affiliation. When the colonial subject subordinates has own identity and values to Western ones in the novel, he imposes a kind of psychological liminality on people around him as well. (12)

Thus Jemubhai was able to recognise the disturbances that haunted him all these years. He realises that he had wasted all his life without any help to others and to himself. It is the same case with that of Ratan where both the protagonists were not the only reason behind their downfall. It is obviously the society and environment they lived which dominated and influenced them in their every step.

The reason for Ratan and Jemu's pathetic situation is their loss of self which is very vital for any individual to live a socially responsible life of values, ideals and goals. Self according to Kohut is the essence of a person's psychological being and consists of feelings, thoughts, and attitudes toward oneself and the world. Kohut conceptualised the self as a mental system that systematises a person's subjective awareness and experience in relation to a set of developmental needs. Kohut called these needs "selfobject needs" because they are related with sustaining the self. In the case of Ratan and Billy, they do not possess any subjective awareness of their action, deeds and its consequences as they did not acquire the developmental needs which is the life source to sustain the self. Erez Banai, Mario Mikulincer and Phillip R. Shaver comment that Self psychology is a reliable and effective as it is a comprehensive theory consisting of both a developmental model and a model for clinical consultation and therapy. They state:

Seven studies examined the validity and usefulness of central constructs in Kohut's self psychology: selfobject needs for mirroring, idealization, and twinship and avoidance of acknowledging these needs. These constructs were assessed with a new self-report measure that was found to be reliable, valid, and empirically linked with a variety of constructs in contemporary personality and social psychology. The findings supported and refined Kohut's ideas about the independence of the 3 selfobject needs, the orthogonality between these needs and defensive attempts to avoid acknowledging them, the motivational bases of narcissism, and the contribution of selfobject needs to problems in interpersonal functioning, mental health, self-cohesion, and affect regulation. (1)

In Self Psychology, cohesive self-structure is the significance and outcome of normal healthy development along the grandiosity, idealization and connectedness dimensions. In other words, self-cohesion is attained when people are stable, optimistic and posses ambitions,ideals, and values.The development of a cohesive self takes place along three axes: (a) the grandiosity axis, (b) the idealization axis, and (c) the alter ego–connectedness axis. The grandiosity axis refers to a person's ability to maintain a optimistic and steady sense of self-esteem, by developing strong ambitions, and commitment to meaningful tasks. In the normal development of an individual, the grandiosity axis is expressed in the sense of self-esteem, glowing ambition, assertiveness, and achievement. The idealization axis refers to the development of a person's ability to form and maintain a firm and stable system of goal-setting principles which in the normal development of th self culminates in strongly held goals, ideals, and values. The alter ego–connectedness axis refers to the development of a person's ability to express and communicate feelings to the significant others, maintain friendly relationship and become a part of larger groups and organizations. This axis in its normal development is expressed in a sense of belongingness and result in a feeling that one's qualities, goals, and ideals are understood and accepted by others. It is also obvious that the individual whose self-expression is blocked would experience himself as prevented from building a tension arc from their basic strivings (ambitions) to reach their basic ideals (values, goals) using inborn talents and acquired abilities. As remarked by Kohut "This tension arc is the dynamic essence of the complete, non-defective self; it is the conceptualization of the structure whose establishment makes possible a creative-productive, fulfilling life" (21).

It becomes explicit that the development of an individual to a socially responsible and acceptable person highly depends on his early childhood where the role of parents is very vital as the child basically depend on them and try to imitate them considering them as their role model. It is observed if given the infant's milieu providing the requisites for proper emotional development, Kohut remarked: establish an uninterrupted tension arc from basic ambitions, via basic talents and skills, toward basic ideals. This tension arc is the dynamic essence of the complete, nondefective self . . . whose establishment makes possible a creative-productive, fulfilling life. (4)

The acceptability of one's personality, talents, and skills contributes to a cohesive self-structure that provides a subjective sense of stability, and permanence. This self-structure can uphold a sense of consistency and clarity of designs of experiences even under threatening conditions. Additionally, it can deliver a sense of inner security and resilience.. According to Kohut difficulties in the development of self along the grandiosity, idealization, and connectedness dimensions lead to disorders of the self, which leads to an underlying lack of self-cohesion, lack of confidence and susceptible self-esteem. In the case of Ratan and Billy nobody accepts them as they do not possess a cohesive self structure As a result, due to their disordered self, they become absorbed on their deficiencies, incapabilities and failure, and are overwhelmed with pessimistic thoughts and emotions, and feelings of alienation and isolation. In addition, such individuals may be preoccupied with fantasies of excellence and power, tend to exaggerate their accomplishments and talents, and work to avoid situations and people that challenge their defenses and threaten to shatter their pseudograndiosity. This is the exact condition of Ratan and Jemubhai as they exaggerate their success and power. But towards the end, the protagnists were able to refine themselves by realising their pseudograndiosity. They understood what is real happiness, success and values in life and they were able to outwit their disturbances and rediscover their true self.

5

Summation

Heinz Kohut's theories had a tremendous influence on the thinking about the development of the self. It has provided a comprehensive theory of psychopathology and treatment which has articulated a new group of developmental needs and transferences: mirroring, idealizing, and alter ego. The theory postulates that the failure of parental empathy to meet the needs of their children during childhood results in the inability to develop the cohesive self structure that can consistently regulate self-esteem and calm the self, leaving the individual to be dependent on those in the surround to provide the selfobject functions. In the case of the restoration of self, the treatment requires careful understanding of the early failures in order to provide an environment in which the intrapsychic structures may belatedly and effectively develop. John E. Gedo remarks the significance of Self Psychology as:

Self psychology may have been the most influential new movement within psychoanalysis in the late twentieth century. Heinz Kohut, its founder, often proudly claimed that it was the product of his introspective efforts; hence a biography of Kohut is amply justified by the role it should play in clarifying the intellectual history of the field. As it turns out, the narrative of Kohut's life happens to be a fascinating story that may interest a wide public, even those unconcerned with psychoanalysis as such. (91)

Heinz Kohut though in the beginning of his career followed the teachings of Freud, later introduced Self Psychology in the 1970s with *The Analysis of the Self due to the* progression of his work with clients who became increasingly dissatisfied with some of the limitations of Freud's approach. Especially, Kohut was dissatisfied with the approach because of its lack of effectiveness in addressing the narcissistic personality. Hence Kohut began to explore the idea of self-love and suggested that some degree of narcissism could actually be healthy and beneficial to a person's relationships with others.Kohut also disagreed with Freud about the source of narcissism which according to him is the result from a lack of parental empathy, than conflicting drives. Kohut believed that when parents failed to provide the empathic responses to a child, then it would not develop a healthy sense of self-esteem and would therefore advent to other sources to gain a sense of worth. Thus The concept of empathy became an important part of Kohut's work, as it encouraged analysts to impose their own beliefs on the person whom they were treating. Hence Self Psychology places a high value on empathy, or the ability of the therapist to understand the experience from the perspective of the person in treatment.

In Self Psychology, the self is regarded to be the centre of an individual's psychological universe. If a child's developmental environment is appropriate, a healthy sense of self will typically develop, and the individual will maintain consistent patterns throughout life. Self Psychology also provides an explicit and more comprehensive understanding of narcissism, as a natural part of development. While a narcissistic personality becomes of serious concern were narcissistic personality traits themselves are not necessarily harmful. Self Psychology highlights the importance of empathy in the context of the therapeutic relationship as a tool to comprehend and clarify what has been observed, rather than depending on a specific action or deed and therefore considers it to be a vital component of the treatment. When a therapist is able to demonstrate this ability to observe and understand a person's anxieties through their point of view, then what Kohut termed as experience-near observation—treatment may further move forward more readily.

Kohut's principal theories have their implications in therapeutic action as his model of self development can be applied to both healthy and pathological outcomes, and that this model requires modifications in classical psychoanalytic technique. The many variations within Self psychology include elaborations of Kohut's beliefs that have been contributed by more recent theorists. Formulations concerning the self have predominant concern of psychoanalytic theorizing over the past several decades where many different definitions have been employed with different perspectives explored. In spite of the diversity of definitions and multiplicity of approaches, certain reliable themes and concerns have characterized postclassical theorising and mark their difference from classical psychoanalysis.

In the comparative analysis, it becomes evident that the early support of caregivers is vital for the normal psychic development of an individual and also to become socially responsible person with cordial relationship with others. Without gratifying, celebrating and appreciating the child in its earlier stage by the parents would lead the child to develop the disorder in self where the individuals cannot be adaptive to any changes in their life. Thus it becomes obvious that the disorder in the development of a healthy self is due to the lack and denial of selfobject needs in the early childhood of an individual. In all the four novels taken for the present study prove that the protagonists develop disorder in self and the primary reason for the disorder is the lack of healthy relationship between parents and their child. Parents who are supposed to gratify the child and so to build inner security and harmony in them, becomes irresponsive. In the case of Ratan, he gets the insecure feeling from his mother, who lived a life of suffering and hardship.

Billy, Jemu and Sampath never mingle with their parents and always maintained a distance. They did not enjoy the earlier mirroring and merging function of the selfobject in their earlier childhood. As a result they did not possess an emotional bond or attachment with their parents. To all the four protagonists their parents were not a source of inspiration who motivated to set their ambitions and goals. Instead, they manipulated their ideas like Ratan's mother who poisoned the mind of Ratan of money and its importance. In the case of Jemu, his parents did not even allow him to dream of his own, as they made their dream to be his for the sake of themselves and their community. He lived a monotonous life of studying throughout and every others nurtured him. So he was left with no other option except to follow what his father said. In the case of Sampath and Billy, they always maintained a distance with their family, in general with the society as a whole. Belonging to the upper class Indian society, Billy in the name of manners and for society there was a gap between the relationship of father and son. On the other hand, in the case of Sampath his father Mr. Chawla behaved like a typical father always criticizing his activities and expecting him to perform what he says and wishes.

All the four protagonists wish to explore from the chains of their parents.as they wanted to be independent and do things of their own. They aspired for a world with their own whims and fancies. Whether Ratan achieved it in a right way or in a wrong way, he became a government official with all the deals that he underwent where he totally lost his self .in the case of Jemu, he became an ICS officer where he was expected to serve his community by his father. But on the other hand, he was after his career and his improvement. Both the characters where least bothered about the society and the responsibility that they have to serve the people. Instead they took revenge on all their early sufferings and disturbances. Jemu suffered a lot in England due to the racial differences where he led his life and not live his life. He was not attached to anything in his life and this dejection and insecurity is what he reflected when he came back to India. In the case of Ratan, he agonized to set his career and was fed up of false promises as he did not possess an insecure childhood with no money and back up. So this had reflected in his nature of developing a weak self where he was unable to be firm in his decisions and was not clear about his career.

It is obvious that Billy and Sampath are totally dissatisfied and disinterested in the materialistic world and they are unhappy about themundane way of living. Both of them are not happy at home and also at their work place. They aspired for something different as they really want to live a life without ambitions and commitments. They are not in any way committed to their family or the society in which they live. Their attempt to get merged with the society became fruitless as what they see in their society is only the worse part of it. As a result they remain alienated and isolated from their family and society. They are not ordinary human beings with simple wishes and way of living, their aspirations are beyond what one can think where Billy wanted to live a primitive life and Sampath wished to live a life on a tree in the orchard surrounded with nature. Thus both the characters are determined to achieve what they aspired. Thus it is evident that these characters did not undergo the process of mirroring, merging and idealization with the help of their parents and the outcome is that they have developed themselves into an unacceptable personality without altering according to the environment and hesitating to mingle with the society in which they live. It is also understandable that the disorder self is the result of the failure to achieve cohesion or harmony in the earlier stage of life.

In the case of Billy and Sampath, they do not own a sense of belongingness as they do not possess any goals and ideals in their life which are understood and accepted by others. Hence their wishes, behaviours and responses were also diverse from that of others as their life seems to be a search for what they long. Therefore their dreams, wishes and interests are robust. In the case of Ratan and Jemubhai, they too feel the alienation and isolation. But in their cases, they are influenced by the society in which they live. As they possess a weak self because of their social background, they are influenced by others. But they possess strong goals and ideals in their life, but not values. Both Ratan and Jemu were after their career and materialistic life rather than a life of love, peace and harmony. They lived a life of pretensions, confusions and deals which were neither useful to themselves nor to others. For instance, Jemu treated his wife savagely of no respect, love and even basic humanity to her. He was not even a good son to his father who shattered his father's dream of serving his community. To the most, Jemu was not even of use to himself as most of his life he had lived a meaningless and purposeless life where he showed only hatred to others. Though he suffered in England, it does not mean that he had to show the same hatred and dejections to others. Just because he was unable to understand what is right and wrong as he did not possess a strong self, he intended to show the same hatred to others. In the case of Ratan, he was ready to do anything for the sake of his career. He had lost his values and humanity of being good to others. Instead he became fraudulent behaving and treating others only with an eye of some profit and benefit to him. Though he was influenced by the words of his mother and his superior, he gave up his identity because he did not possess a strong self.

Billy and Sampath were happy and at solace in their aspired world as they were always not after materialistic and civilized life and world. When they reached their dreamt destination, they became enthusiastic and energetic. Those who were lazy, lethargic and uninterested in their work, became highly involved, mingled and found themselves in the nature around them. Billy and Sampath who lived an uninterested life of no use to anybody were considered a demigod and saint respectively. Gilly was able to cure diseases and was a king by the tribal people. In the case of Sampath, he was so interested to talk to people commenting and advising them on their deeds as he was able to talk on any topic that interests people. Both Sampath and Billy are not influenced by anybody as they do what they wish. Their attitude towards everything changes as they live a life of their choice without any ambitions and traces of materialistic life unlike Ratan and Jemu. Thus it is evident that there are two extremity analysed in the study: the first is that of Sampath and Billy who are not after materialism and so escapes from the civilized world and lives a life of happiness amidst nature and the second is the case of Ratan and Jemu who are always after their career and materialistic life and so lives a confusion not being truthful to themselves and ultimately are unhappy and could not make others happy.

Both Billy and Sampath are not ready to come back to the materialistic world of hypocrisy and pretensions. Also they are comfortable in their new environment where they felt the purpose of living their life. They are not even ready to encourage any disturbances in their new world of amazement, truthfulness and sincerity as they are so committed and involved. But when Billy was disturbed and forced to come back to his civilized world, he was totally collapsed because even the very thought made him panic and unbearable. As a result, Billy did not think of any other alternatives instead he killed himself. It is the same case with that of Sampath, he was not interested to get down the tree for any reason as he felt the bliss and solace only on the tree which he was aspiring all the years. Commercialization of Sampath's popularity, the separation of the monkeys from him, the people following him and the horror of getting down the tree made Sampath restless. He believed that once if he climbs down it is impossible for him to climb up again. He was sure that his intimacy with nature, the environment and the monkeys were lost because of the people and his family who followed him to the orchard. As Sampath was unable to express his displeasure, he believed that he did not have any other option except to put an end to his life by himself. Thus both Sampath and Billy met with their tragic death instead to give up their desires.

According to Kohut's Self Psychology, Billy and Sampath did not possess a healthy and normal development of psyche as they lacked the self-object needs or parental care in their early childhood. Their parents did not shape and inspire them to possess ambitions and ideals through mirroring and merging. Hence they imagined their own wishes which were different from that of others. As the protagonists could not encounter the grandiosity and idealization axis, obviously they could not develop the alter-ego connectedness axis. It is the development of a cohesive self of an individual of being accepted as a socially responsible person who could develop mutual relationship with others and so could express and communicate his feelings to others. In the case of Billy and Sampath, they had their own barriers and hindrances developed by themselves which resulted in the disorder of self. They could never socially engage, adapt to the changes and live a part of a large group. Ultimately they could not develop a cohesive self which resulted in their downfall of their tragic death.

On the other hand Ratan and Jemu did not develop cohesive self due to the secondary disturbances of social background, inequality and economic crisis. In their earlier stage their thoughts, deeds were influenced by their parents: Ratan's mother sowed the need and importance of money into the heart of Ratan and Jemu's father made his dream, the dream of Jemu. Thus the protagonists were not even allowed to dream on their part, create ambitions and set goals. Instead they were wrongly motivated as the parents were themselves insecure and do not possess the ability to comprehend the self and the selfobject bond and so they did not gratify, appreciate or celebrate the achievement of their child.

Thus the protagonists were left with no other options except to reshape themselves as per the influence of their parents. Hence they could not develop a strong self. It does not reflect their incapability to develop a cohesive self but it shows the disparity of the society in which they live with lots of differences and distractions. Though the protagonists become successful in their career and live a sophisticated materialistic life, they have lost something fine in themselves which cannot be acquired using money and power. Thus it is evident that though the Ratan and Jemu are successful in their career, it cannot be considered as success because what they have gained out of it is only money, power and status in their social life. But they had less courage to indulge in the society in which they live. This revels that though the characters possess ambitions and goals it has to be properly channelized for the right cause and the true success lies only in living a meaningful life of use to others and also to be happy ensuring the worth of living.

A critical situation in their life made both Jemu and Ratan realize what they were to others and they have lost in their life all these years. In the case of Ratan it is the death of his friend, the Brigadier due to his deals and the sufferings of the people injured in hospital due to war that left a deep imprint in his heart. He was able to understand their sufferings and his loss of human values in search of materialistic life of hypocrisy full of deals. Though he was unable to undo what had happened before, he could feel the pinch and wishes to live a meaningful life. Hence to repent for his misdeeds, though he was a government official with money and power, he cleaned the shoes of the devotees who visited the temple. Thus he would like to renew his attitude and give a new colouring to his self. Ratan wished to come out of the disturbances and live a socially acceptable life maintaining a mutual relationship with others. He could revive himself and live for the years which he had missed all these years. Thus towards the end, Ratan was able to develop the cohesive self, shunting all their earlier disturbances.

In the case of Jemu, the revival took place when his dog, Mutt was stolen as it was the only being with whom he was very intimated with. Jemu who was stubborn with his uncompromising attitude and rigid English standard was of no use to others. He had lived a life of idleness without enjoying and celebrating any moment in his life. He could have served the society in which he lived, could have enjoyed his life with family and friends. Whereas, he was different from others as though with money and power he was of no use to anybody and also to himself. Bu the loss of his dog made him panic. It made him bring out the feelings, emotions and love which he had never given a shape in his heart. Jemu remembered what he had lost all these years. He regretted for the ill-treatment of his wife and repented that he was responsible for her death. He was even able to feel the pain that Nimi would have suffered living a life without the husband's support and also with a child. Thus Jemu's revival made him humane with values and morals. He felt guilty for his misbehaviours and this is point where he had realized his self and developed a cohesive self to be a socially acceptable personality.

It becomes obvious that Billy and Sampathpossess the disorder of self. Their disturbances are primary and they never wish to develop a cohesive self. In the case of Ratan and Jemu they do not develop a cohesive self because of their social background. As the disturbances were secondary, they were able to overcome it in order to refine themselves undergoing the process of a healthy human psyche. Thus it is notable that individuals are up to commit mistakes in their life, but it should be a matter of experience where they could learn. More than anything it is unique to live a life of ambitions, goals and ideals where the individuals could showcase their talents and skills. Hence they could live an optimistic life of being a socially accepted personality maintaining mutual understanding and cordial relationship with others. In this way they not only serve the human values, but also can be an inspiration and role model to others. Thus the comparative analysis proves the reason for the disorder of self and the process and development of a cohesive self. Kohut states how the Self Psychology views the self and the selfobject:

Self Psychology sees man as born strong, not weak, because it takes account of the fact that he is born into the psychological matrix of responsive selfobjects, just as he is born into the physiological matrix of an atmosphere that contains oxygen. To examine the baby psychologically in isolation from the selfobjects (who indeed are a part of him and of whom he is a part, from the beginning) would be just as absurd as it would be to examine it physiologically in a vacuum, i.e., without oxygen (which indeed is simultaneously 'inside' and 'outside' of him physically, as are the selfobjects simultaneously 'inside' and 'outside' of him psychologically). Being reflected by the selfobjects (mirroring), being able to merge with their calmness and power (idealization), sensing the silent presence of their essential alikeness (twinship), the baby is strong, healthy, and vigorous. (478)

The core concept of Self Psychology is to make effort to understand patients from within their own subjective experience. That is to empathise rather than externally analyze which help the patients deepen their own understanding of their emotions and interpersonal situations in order to help them try to understand how their own way of understanding things may interact with their friend or partner's way of seeing things.

The theory maintains the concept that people do not live in vacuums and the welfare of every human being is embedded in social interaction. In the case of Self Psychology, the analyst refrains from making judgments. Instead they have stance of constant inquiry about how the patient views his or her interpersonal surround and to be interested in how that surround affects the patients emotional state. Unlike Freudian theories, Self Psychology is a two person theory which validates that, one person does have an effect upon the other. In other words, if the patient has a reaction to the therapist, in this form of treatment, it will be taken seriously and not automatically assumed to be driven by some past relationship with the transference.

In Self Psychology, efforts are made to carefully attend to the patient's reactions, and to be flexible and accommodate to the style of work that facilitates according to the particular patient needs. Unlike the Freudian approach, the Self Psychological approach does not demonstrate total neutrality or total abstinence. Within the Self Psychology model each patient/ therapist comprehensive observation is formed according to the established need of a particular patient within the bounds of clinical work and ethics. For the sake, the analyst is gets interested and welcomes the feedback about what is helpful.

One of the most key differences between Self Psychology and most other analytic theories is in the way the anger and rage are viewed. Freudian analysts see anger and sex as manifestations of biological drives or instincts located in any person that must be tamed and civilized by the ego. In Self psychology, the rage reactions result of injuries by another person onto a vulnerable self. The goal of a successful treatment for Freudian is to tame the sexual and aggressive drives, whereas the goal of Self Psychology treatment is to strengthen a vulnerable self. Also in self psychological treatment one will be able to be more robust, to bounce back from injuries more quickly than before.

A client undergoing Self Psychological treatment learns to monitor his or her life in terms of looking for experiences that foster a sense of self cohesion and self- esteem. It also enhances the client with potential, when faced with things that disrupt a sense of well being, to have the ability to self soothe. Also the client possesses a sense of the legitimacy of various needs, which gives a sense of strength which enables individuals to pursue choices one may not have ventured into before.

Self Psychology is also applied in short-term counselling work. It is suggested that short-term therapeutic work based on Self Psychology involves a stronger emphasis on the curative aspects of the selfobject transference between client and therapist which is a more limited notion of the role of interpretation. The theory is alsoapplied to the problem of child abuse. The understanding of child abuse has evolved and, through the application of psychoanalytic principles, has been viewed as a collapse in the parent-child relationship. Self Psychology provides an understanding of this concept and suggests treatment modalities. The case demonstrates the uses of Self Psychology in both understanding and treating abusive parents.

It is the empathic process of understanding and explaining the therapeutic process of traditional analysis which allows the treatment to go forward and the self to acquire the lost structures in what Kohut describes as a three-step movement. Firstly,there is the analysis of defense and resistance against the emergence of the new editions of the selfobject transference. Secondly, the various selfobject transferences and their working through are unfolded. Finally there is the establishment of an empathic response in tune between the self and the selfobject on a more mature adult level.

In the contemporary psychoanalysis, those who are in the mental health field were trained with a general and theoretical orientation towards classical psychoanalytic theory and one of its derivatives, ego psychology. But in the second half of the twentieth century, there were two major disruptions to this theoretical domination in the United States, they were Self Psychology and the expanding influence of Relational theories which is highly devoted to the scrutiny of the writings of Heinz Kohut and those who have been inspired by Kohut's theories to proceed further in a wide variety of directions since his death.

When Kohut died in 1981, his perceptions and ideas were still viewed as heretical by much of the American psychoanalytic establishment. For the significance of his theories about the psychology of the self represent not only in the new stances they presented for the clinician's work, but also in the many classical paradigms that they gradually in the end came to reject. Hence the transformation of Self Psychology from what the world of American psychoanalysis regarded as a revolutionary betrayal of Freud into one of the major theory of contemporary analytic thinking did not happen overnight. Later Kohut's ideas brought out through his papers and monographs marked his gradual public exposition of a new way to abstract the methodology and goals of analytic treatment. As the quotation from Shelley R. Doctors suggests, however, Self Psychology has become so integral a part of contemporary psychoanalysts' theoretical assumptions and clinical experience, that it may be in fact more necessary than ever before for us to be aware of the historical contexts shaping it, and its current

The vicissitudes in psychoanalytic Self Psychology since its origination by Heinz Kohut are described as differences in three branches: the traditional, the intersubjective, and the relational. Each of these branches claims distinctiveness and a major influence within Self psychology. The advent of Self Psychology was a stimulating moment in the growth and development of depth psychology which began with the publications of Heinz Kohut and continues with the adoption of several of his ideas and concepts. His original aim for Self Psychology is to have an established place within the organised psychoanalysis but it has given way to its surprising emergence embodied in solid group of clinicians and investigators outside of the psychoanalysis. This has been accompanied by conflicts, disagreements and different branches. The fact is that Self Psychology has travelled along distinctly different ideological lines that differ from one another claiming an allegiance to Self Psychology, an origin from Self psychology, as well as an advance of and beyond Self Psychology.

The significant and important issues in contemporary psychoanalysis are less representative of a movement in Self Psychology than of general themes in psychoanalysis. However each plays a significant role in the growth of Self Psychology. In Self Psychology, since fidelity is often more to persons than to ideas. Through the original works of Kohut, his ideas have found a significant place in psychoanalysis. The importance of the narcissistic transferences, the perception of the maturation of narcissism, the focus upon the phenomenology of narcissistic disorders have all entered into the ordinary discourse of most analysts. Hence the evolution of Self Psychology has articulated with the emergence of a number of other psychoanalytic excursions. Thus the path of Self Psychology can be viewed as a clue to the entire postmodern era for psychoanalysis.

The varied branches that have emerged in Self Psychologyhave survived in a competitive atmosphere. Each claims a status that depends upon being different from the others. Hence the trends or movements in Self Psychology are crystallizing out without a particular allegiance to a particular person. Although the theory may be inextricably tied to its originator, Heinz Kohut, its destiny depends upon its use over time. There is no doubt that there are a number of different emphases on the nature and role of empathy, but, at present, there are no crucial differences in its definition and employment. Its popularity may be ascribed to Self Psychology but not its utilization as everyone includes empathy as an essential component within psychoanalysis. Another notable feature of Self psychology has been its altered thought of aggression as reactive rather than primary. The parallel issue that has had only a minority of psychoanalysts preoccupied is that the place of inborn destruction and the death instinct is probably one that Self Psychology has effectively bypassed.

The major theoretical contribution offered by Kohut in his description of psychoanalytic Self psychology was that of the selfobject, and the major clinical contribution was the description of the selfobject transferences where all forms and types of selfobjects were considered and described. Selfobject was originally intended by Kohut to mean another person who served to perform a function which one could not perform for himself which he thought of as a forerunner for psychic structure.

There has been a continuing debate about whether the selfobject needs to be considered as an inner experience or an actual entity. The concept of the selfobject and its reliance on a theory of self-development serve to differentiate it from most of the other psychologies. Since Self Psychology regards selfobjects as part of the self, it extends the concept of the person to include those others who function as part of the self. The self is composed of or constituted by its selfobjects.

The literature of Self Psychology has followed a trend in much of psychiatry outside of psychoanalysis in a pursuit of the modes of treatment. The principles of Self Psychology are used in child therapy, couples therapy, family therapy, and even organizational psychiatry. The pathological states have been examined in terms of their self structure, which is characterized by a form of Self pathology described by Kohut, There is as well a particular kind of interpretive interference that is applicable in the analytic treatment of the disorders. There is a change of the position of the analyst from dispassionate observer and interpreter to active performer in psychoanalysis and psychotherapy.

Intersubjective theory is presented as a field or system theory where the ideas of the theory ask for a shift from drives to affectivity and a consideration of the psychoanalytic situation as a system with a boundary between patient and analyst. The interplay between patient and analyst is viewed as a situation of conjunction and disjunction where both patient and analyst make contributions to the therapeutic action. Intersubjectivists claim concrete recommendations to technique in therapy as they wish it to be a perspective broad enough to accommodate a range of practice. The intersubjective ideas are a call to an increased sensibility that can accommodate a number of clinical theories. The crucial difference between traditional self psychology and the theory of intersubjectivity is that for the latter the transference is felt to have two basic dimensions: the selfobject dimension and the repetitive dimension. The first is said to include development enhancing experiences, and the second to illustrate experiences of developmental failure. The essence of transference analysis lies in investigating the dismensions of transference as they take form in the ongoing intersubjective system and this system is formed by the interplay between the transference of the patient and that of the analyst. From the stance of the selfobject as a component function of the self to that of the analyst as a reciprocal interacting world of experience, it moves on to the next category in which the selfobject is a variant of an object relation and in which the analyst necessarily has an impact upon the patient.

Relational Self Psychology theory is less of an organized movement than is that of intersubjectivity theory. Relational Self Psychology is a model driven by the client's experience and needs. Where it pays attention to how these needs are understood and addressed by the therapist. The relational therapist considers the client's experience step- by- step in order to gather the cumulative experiences of the client for a comprehensive and successful therapy. The theory and therapy is client centered where empathy is given prominence for the therapist to understand the client in their own terms. Thus a deep trust is built of more specific kind of interventions between the therapist and the client. The interaction between the individual and the therapist become encoded within the person is termed as the organizing principles that are assumptions and way of interactions which has become the part of the individual. These patterns are used in the interaction between the client and the therapist which serves as the basics for assessment and treatment. As a result the healing and shifting takes place which targets the emergence of a true self in an individual.

Thus Self Psychology proves to be a developing theory enriched by the views of the psychologists. The theory does not merely provide statements, but it is based on clinical experiments. Hence the theory is applied in therapy, counseling, narcissitic abuse etc. The theory has also gained attention outside the sphere of psychoanalysis because of its extent of implication to individuals. The theory which originated from Heinz Kohut is refined by personalities like Goldberg, Frank M lachmann, Paul and Anna Ornstein, Marian Tolphin and others. There is the International Psychoanalytic Association of Self psychology whichtraces its origins to the 1970's by an informal group meetings held in Chicago led by Heinz Kohut, the originator of what later came to be called Self psychology. From these early beginnings, professionals interested in the study and development of Kohut's theory and practice increased in number. Then, in 2004, IAPSP was reorganized as a membership-based organization. The purpose of the organization is that it retains its foundational purpose: the study, research, development, and practice of psychoanalytic Self Psychology and it responds to challenges levied against traditional notions of the concept of self as embodied in Kohut's original work, IAPSP thus becomes an organized forum in which many current divergent theories about the human mind and its development, illness, and cure are compared and contrasted in order to better understand and treat the patients. As a whole, the theory holds good as Heinz Kohut points out, it signifies the empathic understanding of the experience of other human beings considering it as an endowment of man like their senses. It also brings out the importance of human beings living a socially acceptable life of mutual understanding with the significant others which serves the ultimate purpose of living the life rather than leading it. It also suggests the way to develop a cohesive self or in other words how to live a life of use to others.

Further studies and research can be done on other contemporary theories of Self Psychology like Ego Psychology, Object Relation Theory, Interpersonal Psychoanalysis, Feminist Psychoanalysis, Modern Psychoanalysis and others. Also the self can be analysed not only using the Traditional Self Psychology module, but also the derivation of Self Psychology, the Intersubjective Theory and Relational Self Psychology can be employed. The aspects of modernization, globalization and existentialism can also be further researched based on the theory of Self Psychology. In this thesis, the self is analysed on two concepts: those who are adaptive to the changes and accept their life and those who are stubborn and unable to control their emotion and hence meet the consequences. In further study, characters which possess different traits can be chosen for the analysis.

6

Summation

Heinz Kohut's theories had a tremendous influence on the thinking about the development of the self. It has provided a comprehensive theory of psychopathology and treatment which has articulated a new group of developmental needs and transferences: mirroring, idealizing, and alter ego. The theory postulates that the failure of parental empathy to meet the needs of their children during childhood results in the inability to develop the cohesive self structure that can consistently regulate self-esteem and calm the self, leaving the individual to be dependent on those in the surround to provide the selfobject functions. In the case of the restoration of self, the treatment requires careful understanding of the early failures in order to provide an environment in which the intrapsychic structures may belatedly and effectively develop. John E. Gedo remarks the significance of Self Psychology as:

Self psychology may have been the most influential new movement within psychoanalysis in the late twentieth century. Heinz Kohut, its founder, often proudly claimed that it was the product of his introspective efforts; hence a biography of Kohut is amply justified by the role it should play in clarifying the intellectual history of the field. As it turns out, the narrative of Kohut's life happens to be a fascinating story that may interest a wide public, even those unconcerned with psychoanalysis as such. (91)

Heinz Kohut though in the beginning of his career followed the teachings of Freud, later introduced Self Psychology in the 1970s with *The Analysis of the Self due to the* progression of his work with clients who became increasingly dissatisfied with some of the limitations of Freud's approach. Especially, Kohut was dissatisfied with the approach because of its lack of effectiveness in addressing the narcissistic personality. Hence Kohut began to explore the idea of self-love and suggested that some degree of narcissism could actually be healthy and beneficial to a person's relationships with others.Kohut also disagreed with Freud about the source of narcissism which according to him is the result from a lack of parental empathy, than conflicting drives. Kohut believed that when parents failed to provide the empathic responses to a child, then it would not develop a healthy sense of self-esteem and would therefore advent to other sources to gain a sense of worth. Thus The concept of empathy became an important part of Kohut's work, as it encouraged analysts to impose their own beliefs on the person whom they were treating. Hence Self Psychology places a high value on empathy, or the ability of the therapist to understand the experience from the perspective of the person in treatment.

In Self Psychology, the self is regarded to be the centre of an individual's psychological universe. If a child's developmental environment is appropriate, a healthy sense of self will typically develop, and the individual will maintain consistent patterns throughout life. Self Psychology also provides an explicit and more comprehensive understanding of narcissism, as a natural part of development. While a narcissistic personality becomes of serious concern were narcissistic personality traits themselves are not necessarily harmful. Self Psychology highlights the importance of empathy in the context of the therapeutic relationship as a tool to comprehend and clarify what has been observed, rather than depending on a specific action or deed and therefore considers it to be a vital component of the treatment. When a therapist is able to demonstrate this ability to observe and understand a person's anxieties through their point of view, then what Kohut termed as experience-near observation—treatment may further move forward more readily.

Kohut's principal theories have their implications in therapeutic action as his model of self development can be applied to both healthy and pathological outcomes, and that this model requires modifications in classical psychoanalytic technique. The many variations within Self psychology include elaborations of Kohut's beliefs that have been contributed by more recent theorists. Formulations concerning the self have predominant concern of psychoanalytic theorizing over the past several decades where many different definitions have been employed with different perspectives explored. In spite of the diversity of definitions and multiplicity of approaches, certain reliable themes and concerns have characterized postclassical theorising and mark their difference from classical psychoanalysis.

In the comparative analysis, it becomes evident that the early support of caregivers is vital for the normal psychic development of an individual and also to become socially responsible person with cordial relationship with others. Without gratifying, celebrating and appreciating the child in its earlier stage by the parents would lead the child to develop the disorder in self where the individuals cannot be adaptive to any changes in their life. Thus it becomes obvious that the disorder in the development of a healthy self is due to the lack and denial of selfobject needs in the early childhood of an individual. In all the four novels taken for the present study prove that the protagonists develop disorder in self and the primary reason for the disorder is the lack of healthy relationship between parents and their child. Parents who are supposed to gratify the child and so to build inner security and harmony in them, becomes irresponsive. In the case of Ratan, he gets the insecure feeling from his mother, who lived a life of suffering and hardship.

Billy, Jemu and Sampath never mingle with their parents and always maintained a distance. They did not enjoy the earlier mirroring and merging function of the selfobject in their earlier childhood. As a result they did not possess an emotional bond or attachment with their parents. To all the four protagonists their parents were not a source of inspiration who motivated to set their ambitions and goals. Instead, they manipulated their ideas like Ratan's mother who poisoned the mind of Ratan of money and its importance. In the case of Jemu, his parents did not even allow him to dream of his own, as they made their dream to be his for the sake of themselves and their community. He lived a monotonous life of studying throughout and every others nurtured him. So he was left with no other option except to follow what his father said. In the case of Sampath and Billy, they always maintained a distance with their family, in general with the society as a whole. Belonging to the upper class Indian society, Billy in the name of manners and for society there was a gap between the relationship of father and son. On the other hand, in the case of Sampath his father Mr. Chawla behaved like a typical father always criticizing his activities and expecting him to perform what he says and wishes.

All the four protagonists wish to explore from the chains of their parents.as they wanted to be independent and do things of their own. They aspired for a world with their own whims and fancies. Whether Ratan achieved it in a right way or in a wrong way, he became a government official with all the deals that he underwent where he totally lost his self .in the case of Jemu, he became an ICS officer where he was expected to serve his community by his father. But on the other hand, he was after his career and his improvement. Both the characters where least bothered about the society and the responsibility that they have to serve the people. Instead they took revenge on all their early sufferings and disturbances. Jemu suffered a lot in England due to the racial differences where he led his life and not live his life. He was not attached to anything in his life and this dejection and insecurity is what he reflected when he came back to India. In the case of Ratan, he agonized to set his career and was fed up of false promises as he did not possess an insecure childhood with no money and back up. So this had reflected in his nature of developing a weak self where he was unable to be firm in his decisions and was not clear about his career.

It is obvious that Billy and Sampath are totally dissatisfied and disinterested in the materialistic world and they are unhappy about themundane way of living. Both of them are not happy at home and also at their work place. They aspired for something different as they really want to live a life without ambitions and commitments. They are not in any way committed to their family or the society in which they live. Their attempt to get merged with the society became fruitless as what they see in their society is only the worse part of it. As a result they remain alienated and isolated from their family and society. They are not ordinary human beings with simple wishes and way of living, their aspirations are beyond what one can think where Billy wanted to live a primitive life and Sampath wished to live a life on a tree in the orchard surrounded with nature. Thus both the characters are determined to achieve what they aspired. Thus it is evident that these characters did not undergo the process of mirroring, merging and idealization with the help of their parents and the outcome is that they have developed themselves into an unacceptable personality without altering according to the environment and hesitating to mingle with the society in which they live. It is also understandable that the disorder self is the result of the failure to achieve cohesion or harmony in the earlier stage of life.

In the case of Billy and Sampath, they do not own a sense of belongingness as they do not possess any goals and ideals in their life which are understood and accepted by others. Hence their wishes, behaviours and responses were also diverse from that of others as their life seems to be a search for what they long. Therefore their dreams, wishes and interests are robust. In the case of Ratan and Jemubhai, they too feel the alienation and isolation. But in their cases, they are influenced by the society in which they live. As they possess a weak self because of their social background, they are influenced by others. But they possess strong goals and ideals in their life, but not values. Both Ratan and Jemu were after their career and materialistic life rather than a life of love, peace and harmony. They lived a life of pretensions, confusions and deals which were neither useful to themselves nor to others. For instance, Jemu treated his wife savagely of no respect, love and even basic humanity to her. He was not even a good son to his father who shattered his father's dream of serving his community. To the most, Jemu was not even of use to himself as most of his life he had lived a meaningless and purposeless life where he showed only hatred to others. Though he suffered in England, it does not mean that he had to show the same hatred and dejections to others. Just because he was unable to understand what is right and wrong as he did not possess a strong self, he intended to show the same hatred to others. In the case of Ratan, he was ready to do anything for the sake of his career. He had lost his values and humanity of being good to others. Instead he became fraudulent behaving and treating others only with an eye of some profit and benefit to him. Though he was influenced by the words of his mother and his superior, he gave up his identity because he did not possess a strong self.

Billy and Sampath were happy and at solace in their aspired world as they were always not after materialistic and civilized life and world. When they reached their dreamt destination, they became enthusiastic and energetic. Those who were lazy, lethargic and uninterested in their work, became highly involved, mingled and found themselves in the nature around them. Billy and Sampath who lived an uninterested life of no use to anybody were considered a demigod and saint respectively. Gilly was able to cure diseases and was a king by the tribal people. In the case of Sampath, he was so interested to talk to people commenting and advising them on their deeds as he was able to talk on any topic that interests people. Both Sampath and Billy are not influenced by anybody as they do what they wish. Their attitude towards everything changes as they live a life of their choice without any ambitions and traces of materialistic life unlike Ratan and Jemu. Thus it is evident that there are two extremity analysed in the study: the first is that of Sampath and Billy who are not after materialism and so escapes from the civilized world and lives a life of happiness amidst nature and the second is the case of Ratan and Jemu who are always after their career and materialistic life and so lives a confusion not being truthful to themselves and ultimately are unhappy and could not make others happy.

Both Billy and Sampath are not ready to come back to the materialistic world of hypocrisy and pretensions. Also they are comfortable in their new environment where they felt the purpose of living their life. They are not even ready to encourage any disturbances in their new world of amazement, truthfulness and sincerity as they are so committed and involved. But when Billy was disturbed and forced to come back to his civilized world, he was totally collapsed because even the very thought made him panic and unbearable. As a result, Billy did not think of any other alternatives instead he killed himself. It is the same case with that of Sampath, he was not interested to get down the tree for any reason as he felt the bliss and solace only on the tree which he was aspiring all the years. Commercialization of Sampath's popularity, the separation of the monkeys from him, the people following him and the horror of getting down the tree made Sampath restless. He believed that once if he climbs down it is impossible for him to climb up again. He was sure that his intimacy with nature, the environment and the monkeys were lost because of the people and his family who followed him to the orchard. As Sampath was unable to express his displeasure, he believed that he did not have any other option except to put an end to his life by himself. Thus both Sampath and Billy met with their tragic death instead to give up their desires.

According to Kohut's Self Psychology, Billy and Sampath did not possess a healthy and normal development of psyche as they lacked the self-object needs or parental care in their early childhood. Their parents did not shape and inspire them to possess ambitions and ideals through mirroring and merging. Hence they imagined their own wishes which were different from that of others. As the protagonists could not encounter the grandiosity and idealization axis, obviously they could not develop the alter-ego connectedness axis. It is the development of a cohesive self of an individual of being accepted as a socially responsible person who could develop mutual relationship with others and so could express and communicate his feelings to others. In the case of Billy and Sampath, they had their own barriers and hindrances developed by themselves which resulted in the disorder of self. They could never socially engage, adapt to the changes and live a part of a large group. Ultimately they could not develop a cohesive self which resulted in their downfall of their tragic death.

On the other hand Ratan and Jemu did not develop cohesive self due to the secondary disturbances of social background, inequality and economic crisis. In their earlier stage their thoughts, deeds were influenced by their parents: Ratan's mother sowed the need and importance of money into the heart of Ratan and Jemu's father made his dream, the dream of Jemu. Thus the protagonists were not even allowed to dream on their part, create ambitions and set goals. Instead they were wrongly motivated as the parents were themselves insecure and do not possess the ability to comprehend the self and the selfobject bond and so they did not gratify, appreciate or celebrate the achievement of their child.

Thus the protagonists were left with no other options except to reshape themselves as per the influence of their parents. Hence they could not develop a strong self. It does not reflect their incapability to develop a cohesive self but it shows the disparity of the society in which they live with lots of differences and distractions. Though the protagonists become successful in their career and live a sophisticated materialistic life, they have lost something fine in themselves which cannot be acquired using money and power. Thus it is evident that though the Ratan and Jemu are successful in their career, it cannot be considered as success because what they have gained out of it is only money, power and status in their social life. But they had less courage to indulge in the society in which they live. This revels that though the characters possess ambitions and goals it has to be properly channelized for the right cause and the true success lies only in living a meaningful life of use to others and also to be happy ensuring the worth of living.

A critical situation in their life made both Jemu and Ratan realize what they were to others and they have lost in their life all these years. In the case of Ratan it is the death of his friend, the Brigadier due to his deals and the sufferings of the people injured in hospital due to war that left a deep imprint in his heart. He was able to understand their sufferings and his loss of human values in search of materialistic life of hypocrisy full of deals. Though he was unable to undo what had happened before, he could feel the pinch and wishes to live a meaningful life. Hence to repent for his misdeeds, though he was a government official with money and power, he cleaned the shoes of the devotees who visited the temple. Thus he would like to renew his attitude and give a new colouring to his self. Ratan wished to come out of the disturbances and live a socially acceptable life maintaining a mutual relationship with others. He could revive himself and live for the years which he had missed all these years. Thus towards the end, Ratan was able to develop the cohesive self, shunting all their earlier disturbances.

In the case of Jemu, the revival took place when his dog, Mutt was stolen as it was the only being with whom he was very intimated with. Jemu who was stubborn with his uncompromising attitude and rigid English standard was of no use to others. He had lived a life of idleness without enjoying and celebrating any moment in his life. He could have served the society in which he lived, could have enjoyed his life with family and friends. Whereas, he was different from others as though with money and power he was of no use to anybody and also to himself. Bu the loss of his dog made him panic. It made him bring out the feelings, emotions and love which he had never given a shape in his heart. Jemu remembered what he had lost all these years. He regretted for the ill-treatment of his wife and repented that he was responsible for her death. He was even able to feel the pain that Nimi would have suffered living a life without the husband's support and also with a child. Thus Jemu's revival made him humane with values and morals. He felt guilty for his misbehaviours and this is point where he had realized his self and developed a cohesive self to be a socially acceptable personality.

It becomes obvious that Billy and Sampathpossess the disorder of self. Their disturbances are primary and they never wish to develop a cohesive self. In the case of Ratan and Jemu they do not develop a cohesive self because of their social background. As the disturbances were secondary, they were able to overcome it in order to refine themselves undergoing the process of a healthy human psyche. Thus it is notable that individuals are up to commit mistakes in their life, but it should be a matter of experience where they could learn. More than anything it is unique to live a life of ambitions, goals and ideals where the individuals could showcase their talents and skills. Hence they could live an optimistic life of being a socially accepted personality maintaining mutual understanding and cordial relationship with others. In this way they not only serve the human values, but also can be an inspiration and role model to others. Thus the comparative analysis proves the reason for the disorder of self and the process and development of a cohesive self. Kohut states how the Self Psychology views the self and the selfobject:

Self Psychology sees man as born strong, not weak, because it takes account of the fact that he is born into the psychological matrix of responsive selfobjects, just as he is born into the physiological matrix of an atmosphere that contains oxygen. To examine the baby psychologically in isolation from the selfobjects (who indeed are a part of him and of whom he is a part, from the beginning) would be just as absurd as it would be to examine it physiologically in a vacuum, i.e., without oxygen (which indeed is simultaneously 'inside' and 'outside' of him physically, as are the selfobjects simultaneously 'inside' and 'outside' of him psychologically). Being reflected by the selfobjects (mirroring), being able to merge with their calmness and power (idealization), sensing the silent presence of their essential alikeness (twinship), the baby is strong, healthy, and vigorous. (478)

The core concept of Self Psychology is to make effort to understand patients from within their own subjective experience. That is to empathise rather than externally analyze which help the patients deepen their own understanding of their emotions and interpersonal situations in order to help them try to understand how their own way of understanding things may interact with their friend or partner's way of seeing things.

The theory maintains the concept that people do not live in vacuums and the welfare of every human being is embedded in social interaction. In the case of Self Psychology, the analyst refrains from making judgments. Instead they have stance of constant inquiry about how the patient views his or her interpersonal surround and to be interested in how that surround affects the patients emotional state. Unlike Freudian theories, Self Psychology is a two person theory which validates that, one person does have an effect upon the other. In other words, if the patient has a reaction to the therapist, in this form of treatment, it will be taken seriously and not automatically assumed to be driven by some past relationship with the transference.

In Self Psychology, efforts are made to carefully attend to the patient's reactions, and to be flexible and accommodate to the style of work that facilitates according to the particular patient needs. Unlike the Freudian approach, the Self Psychological approach does not demonstrate total neutrality or total abstinence. Within the Self Psychology model each patient/ therapist comprehensive observation is formed according to the established need of a particular patient within the bounds of clinical work and ethics. For the sake, the analyst is gets interested and welcomes the feedback about what is helpful.

One of the most key differences between Self Psychology and most other analytic theories is in the way the anger and rage are viewed. Freudian analysts see anger and sex as manifestations of biological drives or instincts located in any person that must be tamed and civilized by the ego. In Self psychology, the rage reactions result of injuries by another person onto a vulnerable self. The goal of a successful treatment for Freudian is to tame the sexual and aggressive drives, whereas the goal of Self Psychology treatment is to strengthen a vulnerable self. Also in self psychological treatment one will be able to be more robust, to bounce back from injuries more quickly than before.

A client undergoing Self Psychological treatment learns to monitor his or her life in terms of looking for experiences that foster a sense of self cohesion and self- esteem. It also enhances the client with potential, when faced with things that disrupt a sense of well being, to have the ability to self soothe. Also the client possesses a sense of the legitimacy of various needs, which gives a sense of strength which enables individuals to pursue choices one may not have ventured into before.

Self Psychology is also applied in short-term counselling work. It is suggested that short-term therapeutic work based on Self Psychology involves a stronger emphasis on the curative aspects of the selfobject transference between client and therapist which is a more limited notion of the role of interpretation. The theory is alsoapplied to the problem of child abuse. The understanding of child abuse has evolved and, through the application of psychoanalytic principles, has been viewed as a collapse in the parent-child relationship. Self Psychology provides an understanding of this concept and suggests treatment modalities. The case demonstrates the uses of Self Psychology in both understanding and treating abusive parents.

It is the empathic process of understanding and explaining the therapeutic process of traditional analysis which allows the treatment to go forward and the self to acquire the lost structures in what Kohut describes as a three-step movement. Firstly,there is the analysis of defense and resistance against the emergence of the new editions of the selfobject transference. Secondly, the various selfobject transferences and their working through are unfolded. Finally there is the establishment of an empathic response in tune between the self and the selfobject on a more mature adult level.

In the contemporary psychoanalysis, those who are in the mental health field were trained with a general and theoretical orientation towards classical psychoanalytic theory and one of its derivatives, ego psychology. But in the second half of the twentieth century, there were two major disruptions to this theoretical domination in the United States, they were Self Psychology and the expanding influence of Relational theories which is highly devoted to the scrutiny of the writings of Heinz Kohut and those who have been inspired by Kohut's theories to proceed further in a wide variety of directions since his death.

When Kohut died in 1981, his perceptions and ideas were still viewed as heretical by much of the American psychoanalytic establishment. For the significance of his theories about the psychology of the self represent not only in the new stances they presented for the clinician's work, but also in the many classical paradigms that they gradually in the end came to reject. Hence the transformation of Self Psychology from what the world of American psychoanalysis regarded as a revolutionary betrayal of Freud into one of the major theory of contemporary analytic thinking did not happen overnight. Later Kohut's ideas brought out through his papers and monographs marked his gradual public exposition of a new way to abstract the methodology and goals of analytic treatment. As the quotation from Shelley R. Doctors suggests, however, Self Psychology has become so integral a part of contemporary psychoanalysts' theoretical assumptions and clinical experience, that it may be in fact more necessary than ever before for us to be aware of the historical contexts shaping it, and its current

The vicissitudes in psychoanalytic Self Psychology since its origination by Heinz Kohut are described as differences in three branches: the traditional, the intersubjective, and the relational. Each of these branches claims distinctiveness and a major influence within Self psychology. The advent of Self Psychology was a stimulating moment in the growth and development of depth psychology which began with the publications of Heinz Kohut and continues with the adoption of several of his ideas and concepts. His original aim for Self Psychology is to have an established place within the organised psychoanalysis but it has given way to its surprising emergence embodied in solid group of clinicians and investigators outside of the psychoanalysis. This has been accompanied by conflicts, disagreements and different branches. The fact is that Self Psychology has travelled along distinctly different ideological lines that differ from one another claiming an allegiance to Self Psychology, an origin from Self psychology, as well as an advance of and beyond Self Psychology.

The significant and important issues in contemporary psychoanalysis are less representative of a movement in Self Psychology than of general themes in psychoanalysis. However each plays a significant role in the growth of Self Psychology. In Self Psychology, since fidelity is often more to persons than to ideas. Through the original works of Kohut, his ideas have found a significant place in psychoanalysis. The importance of the narcissistic transferences, the perception of the maturation of narcissism, the focus upon the phenomenology of narcissistic disorders have all entered into the ordinary discourse of most analysts. Hence the evolution of Self Psychology has articulated with the emergence of a number of other psychoanalytic excursions. Thus the path of Self Psychology can be viewed as a clue to the entire postmodern era for psychoanalysis.

The varied branches that have emerged in Self Psychologyhave survived in a competitive atmosphere. Each claims a status that depends upon being different from the others. Hence the trends or movements in Self Psychology are crystallizing out without a particular allegiance to a particular person. Although the theory may be inextricably tied to its originator, Heinz Kohut, its destiny depends upon its use over time. There is no doubt that there are a number of different emphases on the nature and role of empathy, but, at present, there are no crucial differences in its definition and employment. Its popularity may be ascribed to Self Psychology but not its utilization as everyone includes empathy as an essential component within psychoanalysis. Another notable feature of Self psychology has been its altered thought of aggression as reactive rather than primary. The parallel issue that has had only a minority of psychoanalysts preoccupied is that the place of inborn destruction and the death instinct is probably one that Self Psychology has effectively bypassed.

The major theoretical contribution offered by Kohut in his description of psychoanalytic Self psychology was that of the selfobject, and the major clinical contribution was the description of the selfobject transferences where all forms and types of selfobjects were considered and described. Selfobject was originally intended by Kohut to mean another person who served to perform a function which one could not perform for himself which he thought of as a forerunner for psychic structure.

There has been a continuing debate about whether the selfobject needs to be considered as an inner experience or an actual entity. The concept of the selfobject and its reliance on a theory of self-development serve to differentiate it from most of the other psychologies. Since Self Psychology regards selfobjects as part of the self, it extends the concept of the person to include those others who function as part of the self. The self is composed of or constituted by its selfobjects.

The literature of Self Psychology has followed a trend in much of psychiatry outside of psychoanalysis in a pursuit of the modes of treatment. The principles of Self Psychology are used in child therapy, couples therapy, family therapy, and even organizational psychiatry. The pathological states have been examined in terms of their self structure, which is characterized by a form of Self pathology described by Kohut, There is as well a particular kind of interpretive interference that is applicable in the analytic treatment of the disorders. There is a change of the position of the analyst from dispassionate observer and interpreter to active performer in psychoanalysis and psychotherapy.

Intersubjective theory is presented as a field or system theory where the ideas of the theory ask for a shift from drives to affectivity and a consideration of the psychoanalytic situation as a system with a boundary between patient and analyst. The interplay between patient and analyst is viewed as a situation of conjunction and disjunction where both patient and analyst make contributions to the therapeutic action. Intersubjectivists claim concrete recommendations to technique in therapy as they wish it to be a perspective broad enough to accommodate a range of practice. The intersubjective ideas are a call to an increased sensibility that can accommodate a number of clinical theories. The crucial difference between traditional self psychology and the theory of intersubjectivity is that for the latter the transference is felt to have two basic dimensions: the selfobject dimension and the repetitive dimension. The first is said to include development enhancing experiences, and the second to illustrate experiences of developmental failure. The essence of transference analysis lies in investigating the dismensions of transference as they take form in the ongoing intersubjective system and this system is formed by the interplay between the transference of the patient and that of the analyst. From the stance of the selfobject as a component function of the self to that of the analyst as a reciprocal interacting world of experience, it moves on to the next category in which the selfobject is a variant of an object relation and in which the analyst necessarily has an impact upon the patient.

Relational Self Psychology theory is less of an organized movement than is that of intersubjectivity theory. Relational Self Psychology is a model driven by the client's experience and needs. Where it pays attention to how these needs are understood and addressed by the therapist. The relational therapist considers the client's experience step- by- step in order to gather the cumulative experiences of the client for a comprehensive and successful therapy. The theory and therapy is client centered where empathy is given prominence for the therapist to understand the client in their own terms. Thus a deep trust is built of more specific kind of interventions between the therapist and the client. The interaction between the individual and the therapist become encoded within the person is termed as the organizing principles that are assumptions and way of interactions which has become the part of the individual. These patterns are used in the interaction between the client and the therapist which serves as the basics for assessment and treatment. As a result the healing and shifting takes place which targets the emergence of a true self in an individual.

Thus Self Psychology proves to be a developing theory enriched by the views of the psychologists. The theory does not merely provide statements, but it is based on clinical experiments. Hence the theory is applied in therapy, counseling, narcissitic abuse etc. The theory has also gained attention outside the sphere of psychoanalysis because of its extent of implication to individuals. The theory which originated from Heinz Kohut is refined by personalities like Goldberg, Frank M lachmann, Paul and Anna Ornstein, Marian Tolphin and others. There is the International Psychoanalytic Association of Self psychology which-traces its origins to the 1970's by an informal group meetings held in Chicago led by Heinz Kohut, the originator of what later came to be called Self psychology. From these early beginnings, professionals interested in the study and development of Kohut's theory and practice increased in number. Then, in 2004, IAPSP was reorganized as a membership-based organization. The purpose of the organization is that it retains its foundational purpose: the study, research, development, and practice of psychoanalytic Self Psychology and it responds to challenges levied against traditional notions of the concept of self as embodied in Kohut's original work, IAPSP thus becomes an organized forum in which many current divergent theories about the human mind and its development, illness, and cure are compared and contrasted in order to better understand and treat the patients. As a whole, the theory holds good as Heinz Kohut points out, it signifies the empathic understanding of the experience of other human beings considering it as an endowment of man like their senses. It also brings out the importance of human beings living a socially acceptable life of mutual understanding with the significant others which serves the ultimate purpose of living the life rather than leading it. It also suggests the way to develop a cohesive self or in other words how to live a life of use to others.

Further studies and research can be done on other contemporary theories of Self Psychology like Ego Psychology, Object Relation Theory, Interpersonal Psychoanalysis, Feminist Psychoanalysis, Modern Psychoanalysis and others. Also the self can be analysed not only using the Traditional Self Psychology module, but also the derivation of Self Psychology, the Intersubjective Theory and Relational Self Psychology can be employed. The aspects of modernization, globalization and existentialism can also be further researched based on the theory of Self Psychology. In this thesis, the self is analysed on two concepts: those who are adaptive to the changes and accept their life and those who are stubborn and unable to control their emotion and hence meet the consequences. In further study, characters which possess different traits can be chosen for the analysis.

Works Cited

Abraham, Joy. "Vision and Technique in The Apprentice " *The Fictional World Of Arun Joshi* Ed.R K Dhawan. New Delhi: Classical, 1986. Print.

Clair, Michael St, et al. *Object relations and self psychology: An introduction.* US and Canada: Brooks/Cole Pub Co, 2004. Print.

Das, Sonali. *"National Identity and Cultural Representation in the Inheritance of Loss"* Points of View18.2 (2011): 94- 99. Print.

Desai, Kiran. *Hullabaloo in the Guava Orchard.* London: Faber and Faber, 1999. Print.

_____, *The Inheritance of Loss.* New Delhi: Penguin Books, 2006. Print.

Dhawan, R K. *Exploration in Modern India- English Fiction.* New Delhi: Bahri Publications, 1982. Print.

Dubey, Shyam Ji. *"Identity Crisis in Kiran Desai's Inheritance of Loss".* The Criterion Vol 3.1(2012): 1- 4,Print.

Dwivedi, A.N. *Papers On Indian Writing In English.* New Delhi: Atlantic Publishers, 2002. Print.

Freud A. *The Ego and the Mechanisms of Defense.Writings,* 2. New York: Int. Univ. Press, 1966. Print.

Gedo E John, *"Heinz Kohut: The Making of a Psychoanalyst"* American Imago Vol 59.1 (2002): 91- 102. Print.

_____. *The Fictional World Of Arun Joshi.* New Delhi: Classical Publishing Co, 1986. Print.

Ghosh, Tapan Kumar, *Arun Joshi's Fiction: The Labyrinth of Life.* New

Delhi: Prestige Books, 1986. Print.

Gopal, N. R. et al. *Indian English Poetry and Fiction: A Critical Evaluatio.* New Delhi: Atlantic Publishers, 2000. Print.

Guntrip H. *Psychoanalytic Theory, Therapy, and the Self.* London: Hogarth Press, 1971.Print.

Joshi, Arun. *The Strange Case Of Billy Biswas,* Delhi: Orient Paperbacks, 1973. Print.

___, *The Apprentice* , Delhi: Orient Paperbacks,1974. Print.

Kohut, Heinz. *The Analysis of the Self: A Systematic Approach to the Psychoanalytic Treatment of Narcissistic Personality Disorders.* New York:International Universities Press, 1971. Print.

___. *The Restoration of the Self* . New York: International Universities Press. 1977. Print.

___. *The Search for the Self, Selected Writings of Heinz Kohut 1950–1978, Vol. 1.* Ed. Paul Ornstein. New York: International Universities Press, 1978. Print.

___. *The Search for the Self, Selected Writings of Heinz Kohut 1950–1978, Vol. II.* Ed. Paul Ornstein. New York: International Universities Press, 1978. Print.

___. *How Does Analysis Cure?* Ed. Arnold Goldberg. Chicago and London: University of Chicago Press, 1984. Print.

___, *Self Psychology and the Humanities.*Ed. Charles B Strotzier. New York & London: W. W. Norton & Co, 1985. Print.

___, *The Kohut Seminars on Self Psychology and Psychotherapy With Adolescents and Young Adults (1987).*Ed. Miriam Elison. New York & London: W. W. Norton & Co, 1987. Print.

___,*The Search for the Self: Selected Writings of Heinz Kohut: 1978–1981. Vol. 3.* Ed. Paul Ornstein. Madison, Connecticut: International Universities Press,

1990. Print.

___, *The Curve of Life: Correspondence of Heinz Kohut, 1923–1981*. Ed. Geoffrey Cocks. Chicago and London: University of Chicago Press, 1994. Print.

_____,*The Chicago Institute Lectures* (1996). Ed. Paul Tolphin and Marian Tolphin. Hillsdale: The Analytic Press, 1996. Print.

Kohut, Heinz, and Ernest S. Wolf. "Treatment: An Outline." *Essential papers on narcissism* (1986): 175. Print.

______. "The two analyses of Mr. Z." *The International journal of psychoanalysis* 60 3, 1973. Print.

______.. "*On Empathy 1.*" Psychology International Journal of Psychoanalytic Self Vol5.2 (2011):122-131.. Print

Kohut, Heinz, and Philip FD Seitz."*Concepts and theories of psychoanalysis.*" Concepts of personality : 113-141, 1963.Prrint.

Kohut, Heinz, et al. *The Kohut seminars on self psychology and psychotherapy with adolescents and young adults.* WW Norton & Co, 1987.Print.

Iyengar, K.R.Srinivas.*Indian Writing in English.* Bombay: Asia Publishing House, 1972. Print.

Manoj, S. " *Post Colonial India in Kiran Desai's The Inheritance of Loss"* Literit Vol 33(Dec 2007): 15- 21. Print.

McLean, J. "Psychotherapy with a Narcissistic Patient Using Kohut's Self Psychology *Model*" Psychiatry Vol 4.10 (2007): 40- 47. Print.

Mitchell, S.A, et al. *Freud and beyond: A history of modern psychoanalytic thought.* New York: Basic Books, 1995. Print.

Mohan, Ramesh. Indian –Anglican Fiction: An Assignment. Barelly: Prakash Book Depot, 1968. Print.

Naik, M. K. et al. *Indian English Fiction: A Critical Study.* New Delhi: Pencraft International, 2009. Print.

Naik, M. K. "*The Lost Cause of Loss: a Critique of Kiran Desai'sThe Inheri-*

tance of Loss." The Journal of Indian Writing in English Vol36.1(2008): 1- 8. Print.

Narasimhan, Raji, *Sensibility Under Street- Aspects Of Indo- English Fiction.* New Delhi: Ashajanak Publications, 1976. Print.

Pathak, R.K." Quest for Meaning In Arun Joshi's Novels". *The Novels of Arun Joshi.* Ed. R K Dhawan. New Delhi: Prestige Books, 1992.

Philip F. D. Rubovits-Seitz: *Kohut's Freudian Vision.* Hillsdale, N.J. and London: The Analytic Press, 1999.Print.

Piciucco, Pier Paola. "Fictional Technique And Rhetorical Devices In Arun Joshi's The Apprentice".*The Novels Of Arun Joshi.* Ed. Bhatnagar, MK. New Delhi: Atlantic Publishers, 2001. Print.

Prasad, Hari Mohan. *Arun Joshi.* New Delhi: Arnold- Heinemann, 1985. Print.

Prasad, V V N.Rajendra. "The Apprentice Self As A Labyrinth". *The Novels of Arun Joshi.* Ed. R.K.Dhawan. New Delhi: Prestige Books, 1992. Print.

Radhakrishnan, N.*Arun Joshi; A Study Of His Fition,* Gandhigram: A Scholar Critic Publication, 1984. Print.

Sethi, Rumina. "The Unbearable Lightness of Being: Review of Kiran Desai's Hullabaloo iin the Guava Orchard" New Dellhi and London: Penguin and Faber, 1998. Print.

Sharma, B. K. "*The Inheritance of Loss: Kiran Desai's Exploration of Multiculturalism,Globalisation, Postcolonial Chaos an d Despair*" Poetcrit Vol23.1 (2010): 221- 25. Print. .

Sharma, Vijay K. et al. *Kiran Desai and Her Fictional Work.* New Delhi: Atlantic Publishers, 2011. Print.

Singh, R.S. *Indian Novel In English.* New Delhi: Arnold- Heinemann, 1977. Print.

Skolnick J Neil, et al. *Relational Perspectives in Psychoanalysis.*Hillsdale, NJ :Analytic Press, 1992. Print.

Solanki, Sanjay. *"Glittering Ruins of the Past inThe Inheritance of Loss"* Contemporary Discourse Vol 4.1(2013): 137- 143. Print.

Srinivasan, K S. The Ethos of Indian Literature; A Study Of Its Romantic Tradition. New Delhi: Chanakya Publications, 1985. Print.

Stolorow R., Brandchaft . *Psychoanalytic Treatment: An Intersubjective Approach.* Hillsdale, NJ: Analytic Press, 1987. Print.

Urmil "Quest for Self in Arun Joshi's The Strange Case Of Billy Biswas". *The Novels of Arun Joshi.* Ed. M K Bhatnagar. New Delhi: Atlantic Publishers, 2001. Print.

Verghesam, C.Paul. *Essays On Indian Writing In English.* New Delhi: N.V.Publications, 1975. Print.

Wolf, Ernest S. *Treating the self: Elements of clinical self psychology.* New York: Guilford Press, 2002. Print.